T0181978

# Solutions Architecture

## A Modern Approach to Cloud and Digital Systems Delivery

**Wasim Rajput**

Apress®

*Solutions Architecture: A Modern Approach to Cloud and Digital Systems Delivery*

Wasim Rajput
Trabuco Canyon, CA, USA

ISBN-13 (pbk): 978-1-4842-9656-1
https://doi.org/10.1007/978-1-4842-9657-8

ISBN-13 (electronic): 978-1-4842-9657-8

Managing Director, Apress Media LLC: Welmoed Spahr
Acquisitions Editor: Shivangi Ramachandran
Development Editor: James Markham
Editorial Assistant: Shaul Elson
Copy Editor: Mary Behr

Cover designed by eStudioCalamar

Distributed to the book trade worldwide by Springer Science+Business Media New York, 1 New York Plaza, Suite 4600, New York, NY 10004-1562, USA. Phone 1-800-SPRINGER, fax (201) 348-4505, e-mail orders-ny@springer-sbm.com, or visit www.springeronline.com. Apress Media, LLC is a California LLC and the sole member (owner) is Springer Science + Business Media Finance Inc (SSBM Finance Inc). SSBM Finance Inc is a **Delaware** corporation.

For information on translations, please e-mail booktranslations@springernature.com; for reprint, paperback, or audio rights, please e-mail bookpermissions@springernature.com.

Apress titles may be purchased in bulk for academic, corporate, or promotional use. eBook versions and licenses are also available for most titles. For more information, reference our Print and eBook Bulk Sales web page at www.apress.com/bulk-sales.

Any source code or other supplementary material referenced by the author in this book is available to readers on GitHub (github.com/apress). For more detailed information, please visit https://www.apress.com/gp/services/source-code.

Paper in this product is recyclable

*To my family, who have supported me throughout all the projects of my life!*

# Table of Contents

# About the Author

 As a digital and technology professional with many years of experience in both consulting and client organizations, **Wasim Rajput** has led multiple digital transformation projects and directed teams and technology vendors to deliver enterprise solutions. He has also managed multiple PMOs that were established to deliver large programs and projects. He has extensive program management and process improvement experience. He has worked with many technologies involving 5G, IoT, cloud technologies, AI/ML, and analytics, and he has extensive research and writing experience in the area of digital and information technologies.

# About the Technical Reviewer

**Van VanArsdale** has spent most of his life working with technology. His dad started teaching him to program at age 8 and it became a lifelong passion. He earned a B.S. degree in Computer Information Systems from the University of Massachusetts Lowell and a M.S. in CIS from Missouri State University. He has spent the last 30 years designing and building systems for educational and financial services companies.

# Introduction

This book provides a comprehensive understanding of the end-to-end solutions architecture process and the crucial role that solutions architects play in designing digital solutions for modern organizations. Solutions architects are responsible for translating high-level business propositions into actionable steps that result in useful and effective digital solutions that meet organizational requirements. This book covers the various steps involved in achieving this objective, from understanding business needs to designing, implementing, and maintaining solutions that align with business goals.

## A Technology-Agnostic Approach to the Solutions Architecture Process

As the focus of this book is mostly on the solutions architecture method and the overall process, it doesn't focus on architecting any specific type of digital technology or related solutions. Rather, it focuses on the general principles and best practices related to creating a solutions architecture for any type of digital system. It provides solution architects with a comprehensive guide to the solutions architecture process, enabling them to approach their work with a structured and adaptable mindset. By focusing on the general principles and best practices of solutions architecture, the book provides a foundation for architects to apply their skills and knowledge to a wide range of digital technologies and solutions, including cloud native applications and systems, mobile applications, AI/ML applications, enterprise software, Internet of Things (IoT) solutions, and others. In this context, the book offers various examples of digital systems architecture and design to illustrate key solutions architecture concepts and best practices. This can help architects to stay current and relevant in a rapidly evolving technological landscape, and to approach each new project with a structured and adaptable mindset.

The remainder of this introduction introduces the solutions architecture domain and provides a summary of the other chapters in this book to assist you in preparing for the topics covered later.

# What Is Solutions Architecture and What Is It Not?

The solutions architecture process is a critical component of the digital system project delivery lifecycle, emphasizing activities that maximize business alignment and the creation of a target technology architecture for the solution. It is a strategic approach to designing and implementing technology solutions that align with business goals and objectives. It involves understanding the business context, identifying underlying problems, and designing a solution that meets the needs of the business while considering factors such as scalability, security, reliability, maintainability, and others. A successful organizational solutions architecture process thus ensures the delivery of digital and technology solutions that meet the needs of the business and are scalable, secure, reliable, and maintainable in the long term.

Here we should recognize that a solutions architecture process is a complex process that requires much more than just collecting business requirements and creating a technology architecture. It involves understanding the business context, strategy, and processes, and also identifying the underlying problems that need to be addressed. This requires a deep understanding of the business, the industry, and the technological landscape. Additionally, effective communication with stakeholders and the ability to balance technical considerations with business needs are critical to the success of the process.

Once the underlying problems have been identified and analyzed in light of an organization's business strategy, the solutions architect is tasked with finalizing the target technology architecture before the detailed design and then implementation can proceed. However, this process should not be rushed or done haphazardly. It involves conducting proof-of-concepts (POCs), evaluating different technologies and vendors, and aligning with enterprise architecture (EA) principles. This also involves ensuring that the chosen technologies are compatible with existing systems and meet the organization's standards for security, scalability, reliability, and maintainability.

The solutions architecture (blueprint) of a project, therefore, is much more than its technical components. It goes beyond just the technical aspects of the solution and includes how the overall solution will work in business terms and solve an organization's problems. The solutions architecture should align with the organization's goals and requirements and should provide a clear roadmap for achieving those goals. Therefore, solutions architecture is not just about technology. It is also about understanding the business needs and designing a solution that delivers business value.

Accordingly, it's important to recognize that the solutions architecture process is complex and requires a deep understanding of the business, the industry, and the technological landscape. Rushing through this process can lead to suboptimal solutions that may not meet the needs of the business, and may not be scalable, secure, or maintainable in the long term. This can result in additional costs and potentially disrupt the operations of the organization. Therefore, taking the time to carefully plan and execute the solutions architecture process is essential for delivering effective solutions that align with business goals and drive value.

# How Solutions Architecture Contributes To Executing an Organization's Technology Strategy

As CIOs and technology executives strive to deliver innovative digital solutions quickly and efficiently, they face several technology strategy related challenges. A McKinsey report [1] highlights these key challenges:

- Modernizing IT systems for speed, security, resiliency, and reusability

- Reducing technical debt, which refers to the cost of additional work incurred due to shortcuts or suboptimal decisions during technology delivery

- Positioning the organization to fully benefit from constantly emerging technologies

- Enhancing productivity within technical teams

- Leveraging the evolving AI landscape and capitalizing on the decentralized market's available capabilities

- Combining multiple technology trends to create innovative solutions and unlock greater potential

- Integrating AI capabilities throughout the technology stack to improve applications and processes

- And more

A solutions architecture process can help address these challenges by providing a structured approach to designing and implementing technology solutions. This process ensures that the organization's technology investments are well aligned with business goals, optimized for performance, and adaptable to emerging trends. For example, in the context of the above, here's how a solutions architecture process can help address the challenges mentioned:

- **Modernizing IT systems:** A solutions architecture process can help identify the right technologies and design patterns that promote speed, security, resiliency, and reusability. It aids in assessing current systems and recommending improvements or replacements to align with modern architectural principles.

- **Reducing technical debt:** A solutions architecture process can enable a thorough analysis of requirements and trade-offs, promoting informed decision-making that minimizes shortcuts and suboptimal choices, thereby reducing technical debt.

- **Embracing emerging technologies:** As the solutions architecture process involves continuous research and evaluation of new technologies, it can help organizations understand the implications and benefits of integrating these technologies into their current systems and processes.

- **Enhancing productivity:** By providing a clear vision and roadmap for technology implementations, the solutions architecture process can help in the streamlining of development efforts, enabling technical teams to work more efficiently and effectively.

- **Leveraging AI and decentralized capabilities:** A solutions architect can guide the organization in understanding and incorporating AI and decentralized technologies into existing systems, ensuring the business stays competitive and capitalizes on these emerging trends.

- **Combining multiple technology trends:** Solutions architects can identify opportunities for combinatorial innovation by analyzing various technology trends and devising strategies to integrate them effectively, unlocking greater potential and enabling innovative solutions.

- **Integrating AI capabilities:** The solutions architecture process helps organizations identify the best way to incorporate AI-driven intelligence throughout their technology stack, enhancing applications and processes and delivering greater value to the business.

- And more

As you go through the rest of this book, I will provide guidance on the processes, architectural parameters, best practices, and industry trends related to a solutions architecture process that can help address the above challenges.

# How Solutions Architecture Methods Vary Across Technologies

In general, the overall solutions architecture process should follow a general framework regardless of the type of digital technology or system being implemented. However, the specific steps plus business and technical considerations within each stage may differ depending on the nature of the technology and the specific requirements of the solution being designed.

Let's consider the following example. When gathering requirements for a cloud-based software solution, the focus may be on understanding the needs of the users who will be accessing the software through a web browser or mobile app. This may involve identifying the user personas, understanding their workflows and tasks, and determining the features and functionalities they need to perform their work efficiently.

The requirements gathering process for an IoT solution, on the other hand, may involve identifying the specific sensors and devices that will be used to collect data from the physical world. This may include understanding the type of data that needs to be collected, the frequency of data collection, the accuracy and precision requirements for the sensors, and the communication protocols used to transmit the data to the cloud. In addition, the requirements gathering stage for an IoT solution may involve more stringent security and privacy requirements that are necessary to safeguard the data collected from the sensors.

As you can see, the focus of the requirements gathering stage differs depending on the technology being implemented. For a cloud-based software solution, the focus is on user needs and workflows, whereas for an IoT solution, the focus is on sensor and device requirements. By tailoring the requirements gathering process to the specific technology being implemented, architects can ensure that the solution meets the needs of the users and the business requirements.

Similarly, the implementation stage may involve different tasks and considerations depending on the technology being implemented. For example, implementing a blockchain solution may require a different approach to infrastructure and security than implementing a machine learning solution.

In conclusion, while the general framework for a solutions architecture process should remain the same regardless of the type of digital technology being implemented, the specific steps and considerations within each stage may vary depending on the technology and requirements of the solution being designed.

## How the Solutions Architecture Process Can Vary Across Organizations and Teams

It's also important to recognize that although the overall process of solutions architecture, which typically involves collecting business requirements, evaluating technologies, and so on, may remain the same, it may differ due to the way it is executed across organizations and even within the same organization due to factors such as department cultures, structure, and governance. For example, a more hierarchical department or group may have a more formalized and structured process for solutions architecture, while another part of the organization may prefer a more decentralized approach and may allow for more flexibility and autonomy in the way solutions are developed and implemented.

This book focuses on each of the stages of the solutions architecture process, regardless of how it is executed within the organization. The aim of the book is to provide insights and guidance on each stage of the solutions architecture process, with a focus on identifying and promoting best practices for each stage. This ensures that the solutions architecture aligns with the business goals and delivers maximum value, regardless of the specific context in which it is executed.

## How Has the Role of the Solutions Architect Changed Over Time?

The role of solutions architects has undergone a considerable transformation over the years, primarily due to the rise of digital and cloud technologies. This evolution has shifted the focus from a highly technical, software-centric role to a more comprehensive approach that considers the interplay of various technical elements. Today's solutions architects are not only tasked with integrating individual components but also with understanding the broader business context and aligning technical solutions to overarching business strategies. This expanded role ensures that organizations effectively leverage technology to drive growth and innovation in an increasingly complex digital landscape.

To be effective in this role, solutions architects, therefore, need to do more than just understand technical requirements. They must also understand the larger business context and work to create solutions that are forward-looking and aligned with future business needs. This requires a deep understanding of the value proposition, as well as the ability to define and communicate it effectively.

Moreover, solutions architects need to have a comprehensive understanding of organizational processes and how proposed solutions will impact them. This is critical because the success of a digital solution often depends on its ability to integrate with existing business processes and systems. Therefore, solutions architects must be able to evaluate the impact of proposed solutions on various organizational functions and work to minimize any potential disruptions.

# Example: From Traditional ERP Systems to Cloud-Based Digital Systems

Let's examine an example that contrasts the role of a solutions architect working on traditional ERP systems with that of a solutions architect tasked with designing a cloud-based digital system. Traditionally, solutions architects working on Enterprise Resource Planning (ERP) systems were primarily concerned with integrating business processes within a single, often monolithic, system. Their focus was on understanding business requirements, mapping them to ERP functionalities, and customizing the system as needed. They often worked with established, on-premises systems, and their decisions were largely influenced by the constraints of these systems. Scalability and flexibility were often challenging due to the limitations of the hardware infrastructure and the monolithic nature of the ERP system.

Contrastingly, a solutions architect working on modern, cloud-based systems operates in a significantly different landscape. They still need to understand the business requirements and map them to functionalities, but the flexibility, scalability, and vast service offerings of the cloud broaden their possibilities. They can design architectures that leverage microservices, serverless computing, AI, and big data analytics, to name a few. Cloud solutions architects also need to be proficient in managing and integrating multiple cloud services and vendors, ensuring data privacy and security in the cloud, and optimizing cloud service costs.

Furthermore, the advent of DevOps and Agile methodologies has changed the role of the solutions architect. They are now expected to work closely with development teams throughout the software development lifecycle, facilitating continuous integration and delivery. They also need to be aware of the latest trends and best practices in cloud architecture and stay updated on the rapidly evolving cloud service offerings.

In conclusion, the transition from traditional ERP systems to cloud-based digital systems has fundamentally reshaped the role of the solutions architect. No longer confined to a system-specific, integration-focused role, solutions architects now hold strategic, holistic, and continuous responsibilities in the design, development, and maintenance of flexible, scalable, and cost-effective cloud solutions. This expanded role goes beyond its technical roots, necessitating a deep understanding of both technical and business requirements and the ability to align technical solutions with broader organizational strategies. Modern solutions architects must also be future-oriented, anticipating upcoming business needs and architecting solutions that are scalable, flexible, and seamlessly integrated with existing processes. By doing this, solutions architects can support organizations in achieving their objectives while driving innovation and growth.

# Understanding Solutions Architecture vis-à-vis Other Technical Architectures

When designing and developing digital solutions, it's crucial to take into account several sub-architectural domains, including application architecture, data architecture, and infrastructure architecture, among others. Additionally, each digital technology, such as IoT and AI, as well as their associated products and services, may bring unique architectural considerations that need to be addressed. This is where solutions architecture becomes essential, adopting a holistic approach that integrates all these architectural domains and digital technologies, as illustrated in Figure 1-1. As can be seen, the primary aim of solutions architecture is to harmonize the various architectural aspects while ensuring that the comprehensive solution remains aligned with business requirements and integrates smoothly with the organization's technical infrastructure and overarching architecture. Essentially, solutions architecture focuses on the bigger picture, making sure all components work together effectively to deliver the desired outcomes.

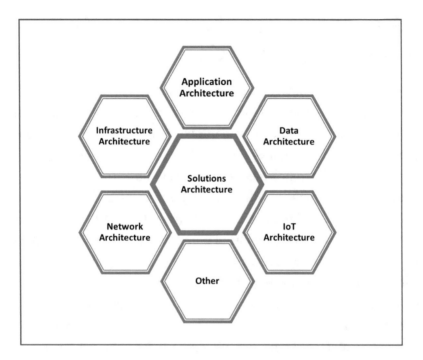

***Figure 1-1.*** *The relationship of solutions architecture to other architectural domains*

Suppose a company wants to develop a smart agriculture solution that uses IoT devices to monitor crop health and AI to analyze the data and make recommendations. In this scenario, the solutions architect needs to consider the application architecture for the software that collects and displays the data, the data architecture for how the data from the IoT devices will be stored and accessed, and the infrastructure architecture for the servers and networks that will support the solution. They also need to consider the unique architectural aspects of the IoT devices and AI algorithms being used. The goal is to ensure that all these elements integrate seamlessly and that the final solution aligns with the company's technical infrastructure and meets the business objectives of improving crop yield and reducing waste. In this way, the solutions architect focuses on the bigger picture and ensures that all the parts work together effectively.

# Focus of This Book

The focus of this book is to provide a comprehensive and holistic view of digital solutions architecture. While there are sub-domains such as application, data, and network architectures, the objective of this book is not to delve into the specifics of each of these disciplines. Instead, the book aims to provide a clear and concise overview of the end-to-end process of digital solutions architecture, covering the methods, processes, and deliverables that bring all these sub-domains together to deliver a cohesive and effective target architecture. By taking a high-level approach, you will gain a deeper understanding of how these different components work together to create a successful digital solution.

While technical knowledge at a high level is assumed, the book does not require a deep technical background. Instead, it provides a practical and accessible guide for anyone involved in building digital solutions for organizations, including new and experienced solutions architects, CIOs, and other organizational stakeholders. To help you better understand the solutions architecture process, the book offers numerous examples related to the architecture of digital systems such as AI/ML, IoT, analytics, cloud systems, and others. These examples illustrate key concepts and best practices, making it easier for you to apply them to your own projects and solutions. By reading this book, you can gain a better understanding of the end-to-end solutions architecture process and how to create effective solutions that meet the needs of modern digitalized organizations.

# Introduction to Book Chapters

**Chapter 1:** This chapter begins by exploring the latest digital trends and technologies and how they are shaping the landscape of modern organizations. It takes a closer look at successful digital projects and solutions, including real-world examples of how organizations have leveraged digital technologies to achieve their business goals. Additionally, it examines the complexity of digital solutions and the challenges they pose, such as security, scalability, and usability. Finally, the chapter discusses the need for solutions architecture and how it can help organizations address these challenges and design effective digital solutions that meet their business requirements.

**Chapter 2:** This chapter provides you with an understanding of the solutions architecture domain, including its process, activities, and integration with the project lifecycle and the organization's enterprise architecture (EA) process. The purpose of this chapter is to shed light on how solutions architecture fits into the overall project plan, how it aids in achieving project objectives, and how it interacts with other project activities.

**Chapter 3:** This chapter delves into the significance of business alignment, its advantages, and how solutions architecture can assist in its attainment. I also examine the essential considerations and best practices for solutions architects to design and implement digital solutions that fulfill the business requirements and align with the broader organizational objectives.

**Chapter 4:** This chapter focuses on creating the technology architecture for digital solutions. It covers several essential steps, including conducting a current state infrastructure and technology assessment, selecting technology stacks, conducting POCs and technical evaluations of tools and services, ensuring solutions alignment with the enterprise architecture framework, developing the solution's target technology architecture, assessing its risks, and documenting the project deliverables related to technology architecture. Each of these steps is crucial for designing effective technology architecture that aligns with the business requirements and the broader technology strategy of the organization.

**Chapter 5:** This chapter provides an overview of architectural frameworks for designing digital solutions. It discusses the importance of selecting an architectural framework, outlining the benefits of promoting consistency, best practices, and effective communication. The chapter explores several industry digital architectural frameworks that organizations can use. It also examines the process of deciding on a custom architectural framework that fits the specific needs and requirements of the organization.

**Chapter 6:** In conclusion, this chapter provides a brief summary for CIOs and CTOs, highlighting the critical role of solutions architecture in delivering high-performing digital solutions that align with the organization's business goals and objectives. It is vital for technology executives to appreciate the value of this domain and how solutions architects can assist in achieving their organization's digital transformation objectives. Additionally, the chapter reviews some of the essential skills and knowledge required to become a successful solutions architect.

# Reference

1. www.mckinsey.com/capabilities/mckinsey-digital/our-insights/new-yearsresolutions-for-tech-in-2023

# CHAPTER 1

# Understanding Digital Solutions

This chapter delves into the world of digitalization, exploring the transformative power of emerging technologies and their impact on traditional business models. The demand for digital solutions arises from the recognition that organizations need to embrace agile, customer-centric approaches to stay competitive. Technologies like artificial intelligence, cloud computing, and the Internet of Things (IoT) hold the promise of unlocking unparalleled efficiency, innovation, and enhanced customer experiences. By harnessing these technologies, organizations strive to streamline processes, gain a competitive advantage, and deliver unprecedented value to their customers.

However, it is essential to acknowledge the complexity inherent in digital solutions. Integrating diverse systems, managing vast amounts of data, and ensuring seamless connectivity across platforms presents significant challenges. This intricate web of technologies and interdependencies calls for a strategic and holistic approach to successfully address complexity and drive digital transformation.

Throughout this chapter, we will explore digitalization in detail, emphasizing the complexities of digital solutions. By understanding the transformative power of digitalization and the need for tailored solutions, we can truly appreciate the indispensable role of solutions architecture in guiding organizations towards successful digital transformation.

© Wasim Rajput 2023
W. Rajput, *Solutions Architecture*, https://doi.org/10.1007/978-1-4842-9657-8_1

# Digitalization and Digital Transformation

Digitalization is revolutionizing the way businesses operate and interact with their customers. It refers to the process of transforming traditional business processes and workflows by incorporating digital technologies. This transformation presents organizations with new opportunities to create innovative products and services, increase revenue streams, enhance operational efficiencies, and improve customer experiences, among other benefits.

There is no doubt that digitalization has already had a significant disruptive impact on most organizations and sectors. As we look across industries, we can see that organizations are not only automating their business processes by adopting certain digital technologies, but they are also reimagining new business models and strategies to implement their visions. This digital transformation is not just a process of technology implementation, but a fundamental shift in the way organizations operate, interact with customers, and create value. To stay competitive, organizations must embrace digitalization and be willing to adapt their strategies to meet the demands of the constantly evolving digital landscape.

For example, when a utility company develops a new business process enabled by a digital solution that leverages IoT technologies, connects to the cloud, and integrates analytics to gain deeper insights into usage patterns, billing trends, and more, it has effectively digitalized its business process. Through this digital transformation, the company can improve its operational efficiency, enhance customer experiences, and generate new revenue streams by offering innovative products and services. Digitalization, therefore, is not just about adopting new technologies, but also about optimizing business processes to create value and gain a competitive edge in the market.

Moreover, we are also seeing new organizations emerging daily, which are built on cutting-edge digital technologies. These digital natives are completely founded on digital platforms and ecosystems and are disrupting traditional business models across industries. Amazon is a prime example of a company that was born on the web and has revolutionized the retail industry. Since then, we have seen numerous other digital native organizations, such as Meta, Zoom, Uber, Airbnb, and Twitter, that have transformed the way we work, communicate, and live. These organizations have a unique advantage over traditional companies, as they are built on agile, data-driven processes that enable them to quickly respond to changing market conditions and customer needs, as well as new digital technologies that facilitate innovation and growth.

# The New Digital Trends and Technologies

The changing market conditions are driving organizations to adopt digital technologies effectively and become digitally-enabled. As the digital landscape is constantly evolving, organizations need to stay on top of the latest trends in order to remain competitive. The emergence of several new digital technologies in recent years has transformed the way we live, work, and communicate, and has enabled organizations to develop digital solutions that streamline their operations, enhance customer experiences, create new business models, offer new products and services, and drive innovation and growth at all levels of the organization. The following are some of the popular digital trends that are shaping the future of business and society.

- **Cloud-native applications:** As organizations continue to migrate a large percentage of their applications to the cloud, many are beginning to focus on architecting and building cloud-native applications. According to Gartner, by 2025, more than 95% of application workloads will be deployed on cloud-native platforms [1]. This trend highlights the growing importance of cloud-native architecture and the need for organizations to embrace this approach to stay competitive in the digital landscape.

- **Industry 4.0:** Manufacturing organizations are embracing Industry 4.0 and smart factories, which are build upon technologies such as artificial intelligence (AI) and machine learning (ML), robotics, IoT, and others. These technologies enable fully automated and connected operations resulting in increased productivity, agility, and operational efficiency.

- **Hybrid cloud:** To make the most of public and private cloud implementations, organizations are actively pursuing hybrid cloud solutions. Hybrid cloud implementations enable organizations for numerous use cases, which include bursting, where additional traffic from an on-premises environment is routed to the public cloud for more resources. Hybrid cloud solutions are also used to set up disaster recovery sites, migrate non-strategic workloads to the public cloud, and other uses. According to 451 research, more than 60% of organizations have already adopted a hybrid cloud architecture and this trend is continuing [2].

- **Hyperautomation:** As the name implies, this technology goes beyond traditional automation by not only removing repetitive and mundane tasks but also automating complex tasks that involve analysis and decision making. This approach leverages advanced technologies like AI/ML and robotic process automation to augment human capabilities, improve efficiency, and streamline business processes. Hyperautomation has the potential to transform how organizations operate, enabling them to become more agile, adaptable, and competitive in today's digital landscape.

- **Edge computing:** This technology is gaining popularity due to its unique characteristics to offer reduced latency, improved application performance, reduced bandwidth costs, and real-time processing of data at the edge. Edge computing represents a shift towards a more distributed and decentralized approach to computing, providing new opportunities for innovation and efficiency across various industries. The technology is being utilized in multiple use cases, such as IIoT (Industrial IoT), autonomous vehicles, smart cities, telemedicine, retail and supply chain optimization, video surveillance and security, and energy management.

- **Artificial intelligence and machine learning (AI/ML):** These technologies are designed to mimic human cognitive abilities, such as reasoning, perception, and decision-making, and to implement them in intelligent algorithms and software. The goal is to create systems that can perform tasks that would typically require human intelligence, such as recognizing patterns, interpreting data, and making predictions. While AI is still a long way from replicating the full range of human capabilities, it is already showing promise in a variety of fields. For example, Netflix uses these technologies to provide personalized content recommendations to its users, while businesses are using AI-powered chatbots such as ChatGPT to improve customer service and reduce costs.

- **Generative AI:** Generative AI, a subset of artificial intelligence, significantly contributes to digital transformation by automating content creation, improving user experiences, and optimizing processes. By generating tailored content, fostering innovation, and supporting data-driven decisions, it helps businesses maintain competitiveness and scalability. Integrating with cloud and digital solutions, generative AI promotes innovation through applications such as customized marketing materials, streamlined design processes in industries like fashion and automotive, and enhanced demand forecasting. Utilizing the cloud infrastructure enables organizations to scale AI implementations, minimize costs, and harness AI-generated insights, fostering success in a digital world.

- **Superapps:** Superapps are a new type of mobile application that offer users access to a variety of services through a single interface, rather than requiring separate apps for each service. Some superapps also integrate user data across all services to provide a more seamless and personalized experience. For example, Grab [3] is a superapp that is available in Southeast Asian countries and provides a range of services such as ride-hailing, food delivery, and financial services, all within a single app. While superapps are more prevalent outside of the US, the trend is gaining traction in the US as well.

- **Metaverse:** The "metaverse" is a term used to describe computer and web-enabled virtual worlds that allow users to interact socially, commercially, and for other purposes. Enabled by the power of the Internet and web technologies, the metaverse provides individuals and organizations with extended virtual spaces on the web to interact and work. Although still a new technology, organizations are exploring its potential use for a range of applications, such as online gaming, education and training, collaboration, and social networking.

- **Adaptive AI:** Adaptive AI refers to AI systems that can modify their behavior based on changes in their environment or user interactions. These systems are designed to learn and adapt to new data or situations, allowing them to improve their performance and accuracy over time. Adaptive AI is often used in applications where the data or context is dynamic and constantly changing. For example, in natural language processing, adaptive AI can learn from new user inputs and adjust its language models accordingly. In computer vision, adaptive AI can learn to recognize new objects or features that were not present in the original training data.

- **ChatGPT:** ChatGPT is a Large Language Model (LLM) trained by OpenAI [4], based on the GPT (Generative Pre-trained Transformers), which is a type of neural network architecture based on the Transformer architecture, used in the GPT series of language models developed by OpenAI for natural language processing tasks, and is designed to predict the next word in a given sentence or paragraph. It is a powerful tool for natural language processing, capable of generating human-like responses to written prompts. ChatGPT can be used to build digital solutions in a variety of fields, such as chatbots, customer service, content creation, and language translation. Its ability to understand and respond to natural language makes it a valuable tool for improving user experience, increasing efficiency, and reducing the workload of human operators. With the help of ChatGPT, developers can create advanced digital solutions that provide personalized and engaging experiences to their users.

- **Robotics:** These technologies involve the development and use of machines that can perform a range of tasks autonomously or with human guidance. These machines can be designed to work in different environments, such as factories, homes, hospitals, and outer space. Robotics technologies are typically based on a combination of hardware and software components, including sensors, actuators, motors, and controllers. They can be programmed to perform specific tasks or learn from experience using techniques such as AI/ML. Robotics technologies are used in a variety of fields, including manufacturing, healthcare, transportation, and entertainment, and have the potential to improve efficiency, safety, and quality of life. However, they also raise important ethical and social questions related to job displacement, privacy, and control over technology.

# Examples: Successful Digital Projects and Solutions

The digitalization journey, although underway for several years, will take more time to reach full transformation. For instance, McKinsey predicts that it may take until 2045 for organizations to achieve full and proper digital adoption in their processes and workplaces [5]. However, by that time, the competitive landscape will have changed, and many companies that lag behind in digital adoption may no longer survive in the market.

Meanwhile, the competition for survival remains fierce as organizations utilize these technologies to develop diverse digital solutions that enhance their business capabilities. Those who are agile and capable of utilizing digital technologies to build intelligent digital solutions that elevate their business capabilities are better positioned to thrive in today's fast-paced and highly competitive business environment. Such organizations can quickly adapt to changing market conditions, meet customer demands, and drive innovation, which ultimately leads to their success.

Let's take a look at some success stories of how organizations have been leveraging the aforementioned technologies to their advantage.

- Siemens has been at the forefront of the Industry 4.0 revolution, which involves the integration of digital technologies such as IoT, AI, and robotics into manufacturing processes. By leveraging these technologies, Siemens has been able to increase productivity, reduce costs, and improve quality. For example, Siemens' use of digital twins (virtual replicas of physical products and processes) has enabled the company to optimize its manufacturing processes and reduce time to market [6].

- Royal Dutch Shell has successfully implemented AI across its operations, with 280 AI projects in various stages. The technology is being used to prevent malfunctions, find new sources of oil and gas, and steer drill bits through shale deposits, among other things. Shell's use of AI has helped to lower costs, improve efficiency and safety, and reduce downtime. Shell has also used a software platform to build and operate AI and IoT applications at scale. One of Shell's main AI projects focuses on predictive maintenance, spotting when valves, compressors, and other extraction or production equipment is likely to malfunction. Another large AI project is aimed at helping the company find new sources of oil and gas by analyzing data from seismic surveys [7].

- PepsiCo, with the help of Microsoft Project Bonsai and Neal Analytics, has developed a next-generation AI solution that monitors and adjusts its extruders, the equipment that produces Cheetos. The system monitors the attributes of the Cheetos using a computer vision system. This system continually captures data about qualities such as density and length of the Cheetos as they move through the manufacturing process. The data is then fed into the Project Bonsai AI solution, which analyzes the data and makes adjustments to bring the product within the desired specifications. The use of computer vision technology and AI helps to reduce the time it takes to correct inconsistencies and allows operators to focus on parts of the manufacturing process that require human expertise [8].

These digital solutions are just a few examples of successful innovations that organizations have implemented to enhance their digital capabilities and pursue digitalization. By leveraging digital technologies, these organizations are transforming themselves for the future.

# Complexity of Digital Solutions

Despite the success of many digital transformation projects, organizations still face significant challenges. Experts from the industry constantly report cases of failed digital transformation initiatives, where organizations have struggled to achieve their digitalization goals or experienced significant delays in doing so. One of the primary reasons for these failures or substandard deliveries is the complexity and scale of digital solutions. This complexity then also leads to budgetary, scheduling, technical, and other challenges that hinder the success of the transformation initiative.

In this section, I will first review some of the areas that contribute to the complexity of digital solutions. Later, I will propose a complexity framework that can help organizations classify digital solutions based on their complexity before starting a project. This can aid in better planning and execution of the project.

# Complexity Factors

Let's now review some of the factors that are contributing to the rising complexity of building digital solutions.

## Impact to Business Processes

Digital solutions can bring various benefits to organizations, but their implementation can also have a significant impact on different aspects of business processes and operations. This impact can include changes to workflows, tools, collaboration approaches, and even the organizational structure. To successfully implement digital solutions, organizations must plan and execute them carefully to minimize disruptions and ensure successful adoption. This requires preparing for challenges such as employee resistance to change, technical issues, and the need for additional training.

It is crucial for organizations to have a comprehensive understanding of how digital solutions may affect their operations and to develop a clear plan to address potential challenges. This includes taking a holistic approach to digital transformation and identifying and addressing impacts on various business processes. By acknowledging the interconnected nature of these processes, leaders can create comprehensive plans that consider the organization's culture, structure, and workforce adaptability, ensuring smooth transitions and minimizing potential disruptions.

For example, the implementation of an IoT system in a manufacturing company can significantly impact the business processes. The IoT system can optimize processes, enhance decision making, and identify trends by collecting data from IoT devices. This can lead to improvements in efficiency, cost savings, product quality, and overall competitiveness. However, the implementation of the IoT system requires employee training, change management, and significant investment in hardware and software infrastructure. Moreover, there may be challenges related to data security, privacy, and interoperability due to the use of different protocols and standards by different devices and systems. Therefore, careful planning and execution of the implementation of the IoT system are crucial, considering the technological aspects and the organizational and human factors involved. Adequate communication and collaboration among different departments and stakeholders, as well as a clear understanding of the goals and benefits of the IoT system, are also essential to its success and its impact on the business processes.

## Technical Complexities

Implementing digital solutions, such as AI/ML, IoT, and Blockchain, involves a wide range of technical complexities that must be addressed in the overall delivery process to ensure their success and reliability. Compatibility, scalability, performance, security, integration, maintenance, and support are just a few examples of the complex technical requirements involved in implementing digital solutions. Each of these complexities presents unique challenges that require a deep understanding of the underlying technology and a commitment to ongoing monitoring and improvement.

For example, when implementing AI/ML solutions, one of the key complexities is scalability. As AI/ML models are trained on large datasets, they must be able to handle growing amounts of data to maintain accuracy and efficiency. This requires the ability to scale up hardware resources, such as GPUs, CPUs, and cloud infrastructure, to process large amounts of data. A natural language processing AI solution, for example, requires a lot of computational power to process larger text data sets.

Another example of technical complexity is compatibility when implementing IoT solutions. Such solutions often involve a variety of devices, sensors, and gateways that must work together seamlessly. Ensuring compatibility can be challenging due to the wide range of devices and protocols involved. For instance, an IoT solution that involves sensors collecting environmental data may need to be compatible with various sensor types and communication protocols to ensure smooth data collection and transmission.

Performance is another critical complexity that must be addressed when implementing digital solutions. IoT solutions, for instance, must be able to process and transmit data in real time to ensure timely decision-making. This requires optimizing the network infrastructure and ensuring that data processing and transmission are efficient.

In conclusion, digital solutions are not without their complexities and organizations need to ensure that their solutions architecture and delivery processes address those technical complexities.

# Evolving New Digital Technologies

Another challenge with implementing digital solutions is that the digital landscape is constantly evolving, and new technologies are emerging at a rapid pace. To remain competitive, organizations need to be agile and skilled in quickly deploying these new solutions.

For example, the introduction of generative AI tools, such as GPT (Generative Pre-trained Transformer), has opened up new possibilities for natural language processing, machine translation, and content creation. This has led to organizations rapidly deploying new solutions that leverage these tools to create more engaging content, automate customer support, and improve business processes.

However, deploying new solutions that leverage emerging technologies like GPT requires a deep understanding of the underlying technology and the ability to quickly integrate these tools into existing systems and business processes. Organizations not only must have skilled professionals who can develop and deploy solutions that leverage these tools effectively but they need to ensure that their architecture and delivery processes can address these business problems.

Moreover, as new technologies emerge, organizations and their solutions architects need to be mindful of potential risks and ethical considerations. For example, the use of AI/ML technologies raises concerns around privacy, bias, and fairness. Organizations must be mindful of these concerns and develop solutions that are ethical, transparent, and secure.

# Integration Complexities of Digital Solutions

Integrating systems and technologies is a major contributing factor to the complexity of digital solutions. Companies need to invest in robust integration processes and solutions to ensure that these systems function cohesively, and that data is collected and transmitted seamlessly. With the proliferation of digital solutions, integration has become an essential component of digital transformation, requiring a deep understanding of the underlying technologies and a commitment to ongoing learning and development.

For example, when integrating multiple cloud services, each cloud service may have different APIs, data structures, and integration mechanisms, which can create interoperability issues when attempting to integrate them. This can lead to delays in the deployment of digital solutions and can impact their effectiveness. Consider the case where a company is using multiple cloud services for their customer relationship management, accounting, and marketing activities. Integrating these services can be challenging due to the differences in APIs and data structures. In this case, solutions architects need to devise robust integration solutions that can harmonize the different APIs and data structures that can help ensure that the services function cohesively.

The distributed nature of digital solutions can also make it challenging to ensure that they function cohesively. Building digital solutions often involves integrating multiple systems that are distributed across different locations, such as data centers, remote offices, or cloud-based servers. This can create latency issues and make it challenging to ensure data consistency across all systems. For example, if a company is using an IoT solution to monitor equipment in remote locations, integrating the data from these remote sensors into a central system can be challenging due to the distributed nature of the solution. In this case, solutions architects need to devise effective integration solutions, which can help ensure that the data is collected and transmitted seamlessly, ensuring that the company can make timely and accurate decisions based on the data.

Moreover, integrating systems and technologies can be complex due to the varying levels of technical expertise required for each integration. For example, integrating a blockchain solution with an existing ERP system may require specialized knowledge of both technologies to ensure that they function cohesively. In this case, solutions architect need to lead a team of skilled professionals with expertise in both blockchain and ERP systems that can help ensure a smooth integration.

## Multiple Vendors

Building digital solutions often requires working with multiple vendors, which can be complex and time-consuming. This requires integrating various software, hardware, and services from different vendors, where each vendor may have their own proprietary technologies, protocols, and interfaces, which can make integration a challenging and time-consuming task. Moreover, managing multiple vendors and their deliverables can create coordination and communication challenges. These issues can lead to delays, additional costs, and project management difficulties.

For example, a company that is implementing an IoT solution may have to work with several vendors for the sensors, gateways, cloud platforms, and networking components. Each vendor may have a different approach to data transmission, processing, and storage, which may require customization and integration to make them work seamlessly. In such a scenario, managing the integration of the different components and ensuring that they work together effectively can be a significant challenge.

Furthermore, working with multiple vendors requires more vendor selection, and managing multiple vendors and their deliverables can create coordination and communication challenges. These issues can lead to delays, additional costs, and project management difficulties. For instance, if a company is implementing a blockchain-based solution, it may have to work with vendors that provide blockchain infrastructure, smart contract development, and application development. Each vendor may have different timelines, deliverables, and communication protocols, which can create coordination challenges.

Moreover, working with multiple vendors can also create vendor lock-in, where a company becomes dependent on a vendor for a particular solution. This can limit the company's ability to switch vendors or customize the solution to fit its unique needs. For example, a company may use a cloud-based solution for its customer relationship management, and it may be challenging to switch to a different vendor due to data migration and integration challenges.

In conclusion, effective solutions architecture processes are essential for organizations to navigate such technical complexities associated with implementing digital solutions from multiple vendors. By investing in these processes, organizations can ensure successful digital transformations and gain a competitive edge in the market.

The above challenges are just some of the complexities associated with implementing digital solutions. Other dimensions that contribute to complexity include security risks and vulnerabilities, regulatory compliance requirements, legacy systems and infrastructure limitations, and more. In the subsequent chapters, you will explore these challenges in detail as I cover the overall solutions architecture process.

# Complexity Framework

As noted earlier, the success rate of digital projects tends to decrease with their increasing complexity. Therefore, it is essential to assess the complexity of digital projects before initiating them. This assessment can aid in informed decision-making, enabling stakeholders to effectively allocate resources, budget, and time when selecting appropriate technologies and architectures. It allows for accurate risk assessment and efficient project management, facilitating the organization of teams based on project complexity. The complexity classification can also assist in optimizing maintenance and support, tailoring training programs for users and technical teams, guiding vendor selection and management, and planning for scalability. Therefore, comprehending system complexity is instrumental in navigating the intricate dynamics of digital solution design, implementation, and ongoing management and maintenance.

For instance, a project of low complexity may have minimal integration requirements with existing systems and cause little to no disruption in current business processes. The technical architecture of such projects is usually straightforward, involving a limited number of components and simpler data structures. This simplicity often means that the project can be managed effectively with basic tools and technologies, and may not require the oversight of a senior solutions architect. Alternatively, the architect's role in these projects could be primarily focused on addressing technical issues rather than extensive strategic planning. Conversely, a high complexity project would demand more extensive resources, a larger team with specialized skills, advanced technologies, and a robust infrastructure to handle its demands. Such projects may involve complex integrations, significant alterations to business processes, and typically require the strategic oversight of a senior solutions architect. This contrast underscores the importance of pre-project complexity assessment in effectively managing digital solutions.

This intricate interplay of technology and business dynamics can create a wide range of scenarios, each with its own unique set of challenges and opportunities. In response to this, we can categorize digital solutions into three broad levels of complexity: low, medium, and high. See Figure 1-1. This figure illustrates two key points. Firstly, it demonstrates that a project's complexity is dictated by a combination of both business and technological factors, along with the dynamics of their interaction. Secondly, it highlights that the rigor of the solutions architecture process scales up with increasing complexity. This insight can assist organizations in planning and allocating resources, setting realistic timelines, and implementing appropriate architectural strategies for successful project execution. By assessing the complexity of a digital project, organizations can help stakeholders anticipate the demands of a project, align resources appropriately, and set realistic expectations for delivery and impact.

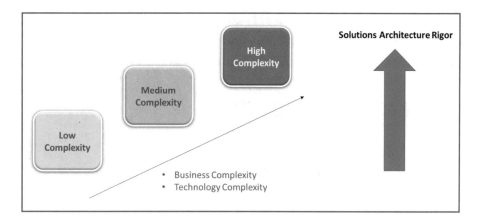

***Figure 1-1.*** *Project complexity and solutions architecture rigor*

The criteria for classifying digital solutions as low, medium, or high complexity may vary from one organization to another due to their unique contexts and requirements. Factors such as the organization's size, the nature of their business, the industry they operate in, and the technological proficiency of their teams can significantly influence their definitions of complexity. For instance, a smaller organization might consider a project that a larger enterprise deems "low complexity" as "high complexity" due to resource constraints. Similarly, organizations with advanced technological infrastructure might view certain tasks as less complex than those with less sophisticated systems. Additionally, an organization's risk tolerance and strategic goals can also shape their interpretation of project complexity. Thus, each organization should tailor the complexity classification framework to align with its specific circumstances and objectives.

The following template provides a set of criteria that can be utilized to construct a complexity classification framework for digital solutions. This framework, divided into low, medium, and high complexity levels, takes into account both business and technological aspects. Each complexity level encompasses unique characteristics that distinguish it from others, providing a clear benchmark for assessing the intricacy of a proposed digital solution. Again, each organization can tailor this to fit its specific environment.

## LOW COMPLEXITY PROJECTS

- Business
  - Low impact on business processes
  - Few users impacted
  - Minimal changes to workflow
  - Low cost of implementation and maintenance
  - Low business risk in case of system failure
- Technology
  - Simple integration
  - Simple overall architecture
  - Low data volume and processing needs
  - Few components or modules
  - Minimal need for system redundancy or high availability
  - Basic security requirements
  - Simple or no need for data migration

## MEDIUM COMPLEXITY PROJECTS

- Business
  - Moderate impact on business processes
  - More users impacted

- Changes to workflow requiring training or reorganization

- Moderate cost of implementation and maintenance

- Moderate business risk in case of system failure

- Technology

  - Moderate integration complexity

  - Multi-tier architecture

  - Moderate data volume and processing needs

  - More components or modules

  - Some need for system redundancy or high availability

  - Increased security requirements

  - Need for data migration

# HIGH COMPLEXITY PROJECTS

- Business

  - High impact on business processes (business transformation)

  - Many users impacted

  - Significant changes to workflow requiring extensive training or reorganization

  - High cost of implementation and maintenance

  - High business risk in case of system failure

- Technology
  - Complex integration
  - Distributed systems or microservices architecture
  - High data volume and processing needs
  - Many components or modules
  - High need for system redundancy or high availability
  - Extensive security requirements
  - Complex data migration needs

To conclude, it is crucial to assess the complexity of digital solutions before embarking on the journey of their design and implementation. Understanding the intricacies of a digital project allows for informed decision-making, resource allocation, and effective project management. By categorizing projects into levels of complexity, organizations can optimize maintenance, support, training, vendor selection, and scalability planning. For instance, low complexity projects entail minimal integration requirements and limited disruption to business processes, while high complexity projects demand extensive resources, specialized skills, and complex integrations. By evaluating complexity, stakeholders can anticipate project demands, align resources effectively, and set realistic expectations for successful project execution.

# The Need for Solutions Architecture

As the complexity of digital solutions continues to rise, it brings forth challenges such as increased development costs, longer development cycles, and higher risks of project failure. In response, the demand for an end-to-end and structured approach to solutions architecture becomes even more critical. Adopting such an approach empowers organizations to effectively address a wide range of challenges associated with designing, building, and deploying digital solutions.

A solutions architecture approach enables organizations to ensure alignment with business objectives, make informed choices regarding technologies and vendors, effectively manage complexity, and ensure scalability and adaptability. By embracing this approach, organizations gain a comprehensive and methodical process for designing and developing solutions that conquer the intricacies of the digital landscape.

The benefits of adopting solutions architecture can be manifold. The following are some of the reasons that shed light on the necessity of the solutions architecture discipline within organizations.

- **Reducing technology investment risk:** With the rapid emergence of new technologies and accompanying technical trends, organizations need to build solutions with speed while minimizing risk. One way to achieve this is by implementing a well-defined solutions architecture process within the organization. Such a process can help to reduce the risk of building solutions that do not meet the organization's needs and objectives by ensuring alignment with business goals and managing complexity. Additionally, a solutions architecture process can help to improve scalability, reliability, and maintainability of the solutions, further reducing the risk of future issues and costs associated with maintenance and upgrades.

- **Inter-organizational alignment:** Solutions architecture as a discipline is essential for organizations to efficiently synchronize stakeholders, processes, technologies, and deliverables, ultimately delivering prompt results. Solutions architecture entails designing and implementing solutions that fulfill business requirements, align with technological strategies, and comply with industry standards and best practices. For instance, in the context of digital transformation, a well-defined solutions architecture process can ensure seamless integration of cloud technologies, data analytics, and AI-driven tools to optimize customer experiences, streamline internal processes, and drive innovation, while maintaining adherence to data privacy regulations and security protocols.

- **Optimizing digital technology selection:** A solutions architecture process can help organizations choose the specific digital technologies that best suit a particular digital or cloud solution. With so many digital technologies available, organizations often face a range of choices when selecting the most appropriate tools for a given problem. While some technologies may be interchangeable, there are often subtle differences that can impact the success of a project. By adopting a solutions architecture process, organizations can ensure that they make informed decisions regarding the selection of digital technologies. This involves carefully considering the specific business problem that needs to be solved and evaluating the available options to identify the tools that are best suited to the task at hand. By doing so, organizations can avoid costly mistakes and ensure that they deliver effective solutions that meet their business needs.

- **Aligning business and technology goals:** Formulating a solutions architecture can help organizations align their business and technology requirements by bridging the gap between the business community's understanding of the problem and the technological dimensions. A solutions architecture process means that organizations can ensure that both business and technology stakeholders are on the same page before the system is designed, built, and implemented. This can help to prevent misunderstandings and misalignments that can lead to costly project failures. By working together to develop a solutions architecture that takes into account both business and technology considerations, organizations can ensure that their technology initiatives are aligned with their overall business goals and objectives, leading to successful project outcomes.

- **Unified vision of outcomes:** The solutions architecture process can be instrumental in helping both the business and technical communities envision the ultimate business outcomes of a project before it gets underway. By developing a solutions architecture, organizations can create a clear and comprehensive roadmap for the project, outlining the specific business and technology goals, requirements, and desired outcomes. This can help stakeholders to understand the scope and potential impact of the project and can ensure that everyone is working towards the same end goal.

- **Facilitating change management:** Organizations need to adapt quickly to changing business and technological environments to remain competitive. A solutions architecture process can help to facilitate change management by providing a clear framework for assessing the impact of changes on existing systems and processes. It can also ensure that new solutions are designed with scalability and flexibility in mind, enabling organizations to adapt and evolve quickly. For example, consider an organization that wants to migrate its data from on-premise servers to cloud-based storage. A well-defined solutions architecture process would assess the impact of this change on existing systems and processes, including network infrastructure, security protocols, and data access policies. The process would ensure that the new solution is designed with scalability and flexibility in mind, allowing the organization to adapt and evolve as its data storage needs change.

- **Promoting Collaboration:** A well-defined solutions architecture process can help to promote collaboration between different teams and stakeholders within an organization. This is particularly important in the context of digital solutions, which often involve multiple systems, vendors, and technologies. By promoting collaboration and communication, a solutions architecture process can help to ensure that everyone involved in the development and implementation of digital solutions is aligned and working towards common goals. For example, imagine an organization that is implementing a new customer relationship management (CRM) system that involves multiple teams and vendors. A solutions architecture process would promote collaboration between these teams by providing a clear framework for communication and coordination. The process would ensure that everyone involved in the development and implementation of the CRM system is aligned and working towards common goals, such as improving customer experiences and increasing revenue. By promoting collaboration, the solutions architecture process would help to ensure that the CRM system is designed and implemented efficiently and effectively.

To address these challenges in an overall organizational process, the next chapter defines the solutions architecture process and its constituent activities within the context of the overall digital solutions project lifecycle. The subsequent chapters delve into each of these activities and practices in more detail, with a focus on maximizing the chances of success. By understanding and implementing these activities and practices, organizations can improve the overall quality and effectiveness of their solutions architecture and better manage risk and complexity throughout the development process.

# Summary

Digitalization has had a significant impact on organizations across various industries. While the adoption of digital technologies has automated business processes, organizations are also imagining new business models and strategies to adapt to the constantly evolving digital landscape. To remain competitive, organizations must embrace digitalization and be willing to build and implement new digital solutions that enable digitalization.

However, many organizations face challenges in their digital transformation initiatives. The complexity and scale of digital solutions often lead to budgetary, scheduling, technical and other challenges that hinder the success of various transformation initiatives. To overcome these obstacles, a structured approach to digital solution design, architecture, and development known as solutions architecture is crucial. Solutions architecture helps organizations address challenges related to designing, building, and deploying digital solutions, ensuring alignment with business objectives, selecting appropriate technologies and vendors, managing complexity, and ensuring scalability and adaptability. Embracing solutions architecture, therefore, can support organizations in achieving their digital transformation goals. The remaining chapters of this book will shed further light on this.

# References

1. Gartner. (November 10, 2021). "Gartner Says Cloud Will Be the Centerpiece of New Digital Experiences. Gartner Newsroom." www.gartner.com/en/ newsroom/press-releases/2021-11-10-gartner-says-cloud-will-be-the-centerpiece-of-new-digital-experiences

2. Yellowbrick. (n.d.). "Strategic Advantages of Hybrid Cloud Data Warehousing." Yellowbrick Resources. https://yellowbrick.com/resources/media/ strategic-advantages-of-hybrid-cloud-data-warehousing/

3. Grab. (n.d.). Grab. Retrieved March 1, 2023, from www.grab.com/sg/

4.  OpenAI. (n.d.). OpenAI. Retrieved March 1, 2023, from `https://openai.com/`

5.  McKinsey & Company. (2019). "Twenty-five years of digitization: Ten insights into how to play it right." Retrieved from `www.mckinsey.com/~/media/mckinsey/business%20functions/mckinsey%20digital/our%20insights/twenty-five%20years%20of%20digitization%20ten%20insights%20into%20how%20to%20play%20it%20right/mgi-briefing-note-twenty-five-years-of-digitization-may-2019.ashx`

6.  Siemens AG. (n.d.). Industry 4.0. Retrieved March 2, 2023, from `https://new.siemens.com/vn/en/company/about/businesses/digital-industries/industry-40.html`

7.  *Wall Street Journal.* (2019). "Shell's Companywide AI Effort Shows Early Returns." Retrieved from `www.wsj.com/articles/shells-companywide-ai-effort-shows-early-returns-11574764204`

8.  Microsoft. (n.d.). "PepsiCo & Cheetos are using AI to transform their product development." Retrieved March 2, 2023, from `https://customers.microsoft.com/en-us/story/858753-PepsiCheetos`

9.  Russel, S. J., & Norvig, P. (2010). *Artificial intelligence: a modern approach*. Pearson Education.

10.   Jordan, M. I., & Mitchell, T. M. (2015). "Machine learning: Trends, perspectives, and prospects," *Science*, 349(6245), 255-260.

11.   Wang, W., Yu, W., Zhang, J., Yang, X., & Zhang, Y. (2021). "Superapp users' loyalty and stickiness: Evidence from WeChat." Electronic Commerce Research, 21(2), 261-279.

# CHAPTER 2

# The Digital Solutions Architecture Process and Activities

The objective of this chapter is to provide insight into the solutions architecture domain, which includes its process, activities, and integration within the project lifecycle and the organization's enterprise architecture (EA) process. The purpose of this is to help you understand how solutions architecture fits into the project's overall plan, how it contributes to achieving project objectives, and how it integrates with other project activities. Additionally, solutions architecture is essential for ensuring that digital solutions align with the organization's broader strategic goals and architectural principles.

## What Is Solutions Architecture?

In this section, I delve into a more detailed explanation of solutions architecture. Often, the term "solutions architecture" is primarily associated with a tangible deliverable including a set of technical documents, such as architecture diagrams. However, this perspective is rather narrow and doesn't encompass the full breadth of what solutions architecture entails.

Solutions architecture is not just a set of deliverables. It is also a comprehensive process that involves strategic planning, problem solving, and collaboration, along with the creation of technical deliverables. Essentially, it's a discipline that encompasses both a detailed process and a series of technical deliverables. Now, let's examine both these aspects in greater depth.

On one hand, the **process** aspect involves a sequence of steps carried out by a solutions architect. This begins with understanding the business problem or goal, followed by requirements gathering, analysis, and solution design. Then, the proposed solution is validated, and finally, the detailed solution design is documented. This process requires the architect to have a deep understanding of both the technical and business domains and to effectively communicate and collaborate with various stakeholders.

On the other hand, the **deliverables** from solutions architecture typically include various technical artifacts, like system diagrams, data models, and technical specifications. These documents provide a detailed view of the proposed solution, its components, their interactions, and how they work together to solve the business problem or achieve the business goal. They serve as a guide for the implementation team, while also acting as a reference for future improvements or changes.

There are several definitions for solutions architect in the industry. Let's review some of them. According to The Open Group, solutions architecture is a discipline that "typically applies to a single project or project release, assisting in the translation of requirements into a solution vision, high-level business and/or IT system specifications, and a portfolio of implementation tasks" [1]. On the other hand, Gartner defines it as "an architectural description of a specific solution" that "combines guidance from different enterprise architecture viewpoints (business, information, and technical), as well as from the enterprise solution architecture (ESA)" [2].

In the following discussion, I will delve into both the **process** and **deliverable** dimensions that encompass the concept of solutions architecture. First, let's cover the overall process aspects of solutions architecture.

- Solutions architecture **plays a critical role in aligning the technical solution with the organization's business goals and strategies**. It ensures that the system not only meets the immediate technical requirements but also supports the organization's strategic objectives. By understanding the business context and requirements, the solutions architect can design a system that delivers the desired business outcomes, such as improving operational efficiency, enhancing customer experience, or enabling new business models. This alignment between the technical solution and business goals is a key factor in the success of any digital transformation initiative.

  For instance, consider a healthcare organization aiming to improve patient experiences and streamline operations. The strategic objectives might include reducing wait times, enhancing patient engagement, and improving data management. The solutions architect, in this context, would design a digital solution, such as a comprehensive patient management system, that aligns with these goals. The system could include features like online appointment booking to decrease wait times, a patient portal for enhanced engagement, and a robust data management system for efficient handling of patient records. By aligning the technical solution with the organization's business goals, the solutions architect ensures the system not only meets immediate technical needs but also furthers the strategic objectives, ultimately contributing to the success of the organization's digital transformation initiative.

- A solutions architecture **defines the principles and guidelines for the system's design and evolution**. It provides a set of design principles that drives decisions about the system, helping to ensure consistency and coherence across different parts of the solution. These principles also guide the system's evolution and adaptation to changes in the organization's business requirements, technology environment, and other factors. By adhering to these principles, the development team can create a solution that is robust, flexible, and capable of meeting future needs.

For example, in the context of developing an e-commerce platform, the principles include modularity, which ensures system stability and ease of updates; scalability, which prepares the platform to handle increasing customer demands; security, which protects sensitive data and transactions; interoperability, which facilitates integration with external systems; and user-centric design, which prioritizes a positive customer experience. As the platform evolves—perhaps due to business expansion or the emergence of new technologies—these principles maintain system robustness, flexibility, and alignment with objectives. For instance, if global expansion occurs, the principles of scalability and interoperability would guide the platform's adaptation to handle new currencies, languages, and integrations with different payment or shipping providers.

- Solutions architecture **facilitates decision-making during the system's design and implementation**. It provides a framework that helps stakeholders make informed decisions about technology choices, design options, tradeoffs, and other key aspects of the system. This reduces ambiguity and uncertainty, leading to better decision-making and a more successful project outcome.

  For instance, consider the development of a mobile banking application. The solutions architecture for this project would provide a structured approach to decision-making regarding key aspects of the system. It would outline potential technology choices, such as whether to develop the app natively for iOS and Android or to use a cross-platform solution. It would provide insights into design options, like user interface elements or the flow of transactions within the app. The solutions architecture might also help stakeholders understand necessary trade-offs, such as balancing advanced security measures with user convenience. This detailed framework minimizes uncertainty and facilitates informed decision-making, which can enhance the overall success of the project, leading to a mobile banking app that effectively meets user needs and business objectives.

- Solutions architecture **considers and contributes to the system's scalability, resilience, security, and other non-functional requirements**. By considering these factors during the design phase, the solutions architect can ensure that the system can handle increasing volumes of data or users, recover from failures or disruptions, and protect against security threats. These are critical aspects that ensure the system's long-term viability and success in a dynamic and challenging business environment.

Consider an AI-powered customer service chatbot being developed for a large e-commerce platform. The solutions architecture would play a crucial role in addressing the system's scalability, resilience, and security. For scalability, the architecture might incorporate cloud-based machine learning models that can handle increasing volumes of user interactions, especially during peak shopping periods. For resilience, the architecture might include failover mechanisms and redundancy to ensure the chatbot system remains functional even if one component fails or if there's a disruption in the service. Regarding security, the solutions architect might employ encryption for data at rest and in transit, as well as anonymization techniques to protect user data, given that the chatbot will be handling sensitive customer information. By integrating these non-functional requirements into the system's architecture from the beginning, the solutions architect ensures the long-term viability and success of the AI chatbot in a dynamic and challenging e-commerce environment.

Next, let's explore the deliverables dimension of solutions architecture.

- A solutions architecture deliverable **refers to a technical diagram, which serves as a visual representation of the technical design of a solution**, providing a common language for the entire team to reference throughout the project. This fosters a shared understanding of the system's design, functionality, and requirements among all stakeholders. Additionally, the diagram facilitates effective communication and collaboration between different teams, including developers, testers, and project managers, ensuring alignment and shared goals. Overall, the solutions architecture diagram serves as a crucial reference document during the design and implementation phases, promoting a smooth and efficient progression of the project.

For example, consider the development of a cloud-based inventory management system for a retail company. The solutions architecture diagram would visually depict the system's components, such as the user interface, database, data flows, and integration with external systems. It would provide a clear overview of the system's structure and interactions, enabling developers to understand how different parts of the system connect and ensuring testers comprehend the expected functionality. Project managers can also refer to the diagram to track progress and ensure the project remains aligned with the intended design. By having a centralized visual representation, the solutions architecture diagram facilitates effective communication and collaboration among the development, testing, and management teams, ensuring a successful implementation of the cloud-based inventory management system.

- A solutions architecture deliverable **encompasses the comprehensive set of technical elements and building blocks involved in the design and development of a digital system**. This encompasses applications, databases, network elements, and various hardware and software components that collectively constitute the overall technical solution. By having a well-defined architecture description that illustrates these components, a clear understanding of the system's structure and functionality is achieved, facilitating effective communication and collaboration among stakeholders. This clarity in architecture also allows for easy adaptability and modification of the system as requirements evolve, resulting in time and effort savings in the long term while ensuring alignment with the needs of all stakeholders.

  For example, consider the development of an e-learning platform. The solutions architecture would entail identifying and defining the applications required for user interactions, such as the learning management system, content delivery systems, and assessment tools. Additionally, the architecture would encompass databases to store user data, content repositories, and analytics databases. Network elements like servers, load balancers, and firewalls would be considered, along with other hardware and software components needed for the platform's operation. By having a clear architecture description, all stakeholders involved in the project, including instructional designers, developers, and administrators, can understand the system's structure and collaborate effectively to ensure the platform's successful implementation and ongoing evolution to meet the needs of learners and educators.

- A solutions architecture deliverable **serves to visually depict the interfaces and relationships between different hardware and software building blocks within a digital system**. It showcases how these components interact, the flow of data between them, and their integration with external systems or platforms. The architecture also brings attention to the dependencies, constraints, and limitations that influence the overall design and implementation of the solution. This comprehensive overview plays a critical role in mitigating risks and preventing expensive errors during the implementation phase.

For example, consider the development of a smart home automation system. The solutions architecture deliverable would illustrate how the various components, such as sensors, actuators, controllers, and the central smart hub, interact with each other. It would showcase how data flows between these components to enable automated functions like lighting control, temperature adjustment, and security monitoring. The architecture would also outline any dependencies on external systems, such as integration with a voice assistant platform or mobile app. By visualizing these relationships and dependencies, the solutions architecture helps identify potential bottlenecks, compatibility issues, and constraints, ensuring a smoother implementation and minimizing the risk of errors or malfunctions in the smart home automation system.

- The solutions architecture deliverable also **serves to depict the intended behavior and functionality of the system**. It encompasses how the system will respond to different application scenarios and how it will perform under varying workloads and usage patterns. By offering a holistic perspective of the system's behavior and structure, the solutions architecture plays a vital role in ensuring that the system aligns with the organization's requirements for function The solutions architecture also serves to illustrate the desired behavior and functionality of a supply chain system. It encompasses how the system will respond to various supply chain scenarios, such as demand fluctuations, inventory management, order fulfillment, and logistics coordination. By providing a comprehensive view of the system's behavior and structure, the solutions architecture ensures that the system meets the organization's requirements for functionality, security, performance, and other critical factors.

  For example, consider the development of a cloud-based supply chain system for a retail company. The solutions architecture would outline how the system handles different scenarios, including order processing, inventory tracking, supplier management, and distribution logistics. It would showcase the expected behavior and functionality of the system under varying workloads, such as managing peak shopping seasons or sudden spikes in demand. The architecture would also encompass features like real-time visibility of inventory levels, automated replenishment processes, and secure data exchange with suppliers and logistics partners. By

having a comprehensive view of the system's behavior
and construction, the solutions architecture ensures
that the cloud-based supply chain system meets
the organization's requirements for efficient, agile,
and cost-effective supply chain operations, security,
performance, and other essential factors.

In conclusion, we can say that solutions architecture is both a process as well as a collection of deliverables that play a vital role in bridging an organization's strategic objectives with the practical realization of those objectives. As a process, it encompasses various activities from requirement gathering to system testing, ensuring effective design and implementation. The deliverables, in the form of blueprints and architecture diagrams, provide concrete outputs depicting different elements of the system and their interconnections. These blueprints guide the project through development, implementation, and maintenance stages, offering critical insights into the technical and operational components. Also, by aligning the system with business goals and existing technological infrastructure, solutions architecture ensures a robust, scalable solution that seamlessly integrates with the organization's objectives.

# Solutions Architecture Activities vs. the Project Lifecycle

Let's now review the project lifecycle of a typical digital solution, which outlines the various organizational and project activities required to deliver the desired digital solution. Typically, digital solutions are delivered as part of an organizational project or program. Projects and programs serve as the means to drive change within organizations, providing a structured approach to initiating, planning, executing, and closing out specific initiatives aimed at achieving defined objectives or outcomes.

Successfully completing projects and programs can help organizations reach their strategic goals, enhance their competitive position, and improve overall performance. While there are distinctions between projects and programs, for the purpose of this book, I will use the terms interchangeably.

A project or program manager is usually responsible for overseeing the entire program, from its inception to its implementation. Their role involves allocating resources and managing project activities to ensure the digital solution is delivered to the organization's customers within the approved budget, using established project management methodologies.

On the other hand, the solutions architect primarily focuses on creating the target technical architecture of the solution and ensuring its alignment with the organization's overall EA and business objectives. In this chapter, I will first introduce the activities related to a typical digital project lifecycle. Afterward, I will shift the focus to the activities specific to solutions architecture that occur within the broader project lifecycle.

# Typical Project Lifecycle Activities

A typical project lifecycle for a digital solution involves several stages and activities, from its inception to completion. At a high level, it typically includes the phases of initiation, requirements and analysis, design, build, testing, deployment, and operations/maintenance. The following are the typical phases and sub-activities related to the high-level steps mentioned earlier. While each project modifies these steps depending on circumstances, these are the most common steps.

1. **Initiation/problem definition**

   a. Start with a business problem

   b. Define the initial problem statement

   c. Identify and define the program scope

    d. Finalize a program charter along with delineating the overall value to the program

    e. Identify program stakeholders

    f. Conduct business and technical feasibility studies

    g. Finalize funding resources

    h. Create an initial program roadmap and plan

    i. Identify the overarching digital strategy that will drive the design and delivery of the digital solution (Input to the solutions architecture process)

    j. Define the overall program roadmap for various key deliverables and milestones

2. **Requirements and analysis**

    a. Gather functional requirements

    b. Gather/derive non-functional requirements

    c. Validate requirements

3. **Design and target technical architecture**

    a. Define an application, data, and network strategy for the program

    b. Develop a high-level design or target architecture of the solution

    c. Develop a detailed or low-level design

    d. Conduct POCs/assess technical feasibility

4. **Build/development**

    a. Software development

    b. System implementation activities

5.  **Testing** (includes sub-phases such as test planning, test case development, test data preparation, test execution, defect tracking, user acceptance testing, and regression testing)

6.  **Deployment/implementation** (involves pre-deployment planning, build and release management, deployment execution, verification and validation, and post-deployment support)

7.  **Operations and maintenance** (involves issue identification and reporting, issue analysis and prioritization, issue resolution, change management, and system monitoring and optimization)

# Are "Design" and "Architecture" the Same?

Although the above shows the steps of design and architecture in one phase, there is a distinction between them. This distinction is a common topic of discussion in the industry [3]. Many people tend to use these terms interchangeably, but this is incorrect. Architecture typically refers to the high-level structure and organization of a system. It defines the major components of a system, their relationships, and how they interact with each other. It sets the strategic direction and the principles that guide system evolution over time. Architecture is concerned with making sure the system meets the technical and business requirements while aligning with the organization's strategic goals.

Design, on the other hand, focuses more on the specific details of system components and their interfaces. It is the phase where architects and engineers translate the high-level architectural principles into detailed, practical specifications for system components. These components can include software modules, databases, user interfaces, and network configurations, among others. Design includes making decisions on the best practices, methodologies, and technologies to use in building the system. It is concerned with the "how" of the system, such as how it will function, how it will be implemented, how it will handle specific tasks and problems. This is where the real-world constraints such as cost, time, existing infrastructure, and resources come into play.

To recap and clarify, here are some key differences between architecture and design:

- Architecture, being broader in scope, deals with high-level considerations, while design is more specific and granular. Crafting an architecture requires adopting a high-level, comprehensive view of the overall system, encapsulating all business requirements and corresponding functions. In contrast, design delves into the details of each subsystem or component.

- Architecture often centers on the system's overall structure and strategic design. It may incorporate an awareness of a range of technologies, but isn't always tied to a specific one, offering a level of technology-agnosticism. However, specific contexts or requirements, like using cloud technologies, might necessitate more particular architectural decisions. For instance, if AWS is the intended platform, the architecture may need to take into account AWS services, capabilities, and best practices. Conversely, the design phase requires an in-depth understanding of the chosen technologies, such as knowing how to optimally leverage AWS services, understanding the platform's specific quirks, and utilizing its data management options to effectively create a solution.

- An architecture, in itself, does not provide sufficient detail to commence system construction. Extensive design work is needed to traverse various phases and delve into specifics before tangible development and implementation can get underway.

- In industry terminology, architecture is sometimes referred to as "high-level design" and the more detailed design is referred to as "low-level design."

## Example: Architecture vs. Design

Let's further clarify the above by considering the example of a large cloud-based e-commerce system that includes features like user management, product catalog, shopping cart, payment processing, and order management.

## Architecture

- **System organization:** The architecture would define the high-level structure of the system, which might include a front-end application for users, backend services for managing users, products, shopping cart, and orders, and separate services or microservices for payment processing.

- **Technology stack:** The architecture would also specify the technology stack, such as using AWS as the cloud provider, a serverless architecture with AWS Lambda for the backend services, React for the front-end application, and DynamoDB for the database.

- **Data management:** The architecture would define how data is stored, processed, and accessed in the system, such as using a NoSQL database like DynamoDB for scalable data storage and AWS S3 for storing product images.

- **Security:** The architecture would define the overall security approach, such as using Amazon Cognito for user authentication and authorization, encrypting sensitive data, and ensuring all communications are done over HTTPS.

- **Scalability and performance:** The architecture would consider how the system can scale to handle increased load, such as using AWS Auto Scaling to adjust the number of running instances based on demand.

# Design

Let's now consider design types of issues.

- **User interface:** The design would specify the details of the user interface, such as how products are displayed on the screen, how users navigate the product catalog, and how they add items to the shopping cart and complete their purchase.

- **APIs:** The design would define the specifics of the APIs provided by the backend services, such as the endpoints, request/response formats, and error handling.

- **Data models:** The design would define the detailed data models, such as what attributes a product or a user has and how they are stored in the database.

- **Business logic:** The design would specify how the various pieces of business logic are implemented, such as how the total price of the shopping cart is calculated or how inventory is updated when a purchase is made.

- **Integration:** The design would detail how the system integrates with external systems, such as how it calls the payment gateway API to process payments.

In essence, architecture provides the high-level blueprint and strategic decisions about the system, while design fills in the specifics of how each part of the system will work and how it will be implemented. Both are critical for building a successful, scalable, and secure system.

In summary, although architecture and design are often used interchangeably, they are two distinct activities. Architecture provides the foundation for the design work to begin, and the design phase is where the actual system components are detailed and then developed later in the development phase.

# Typical Solutions Architecture Activities

As previously highlighted, solution architecture activities operate within the broader context of the overall project lifecycle. They represent a specific subset of the total project lifecycle. Although these tasks might not always be directly identified as "solution architecture specific," solution architects, in partnership with project managers, steer these tasks to realize the desired technical architecture of the project. Given the crucial role these tasks play in molding the technical direction and outcome of the project, we can justifiably classify them as "solution architecture specific."

These tasks and activities include gathering and finalizing business requirements, aligning the proposed solution with business objectives, devising the technical architecture, defining a delivery process specific to digital solutions, and establishing the architectural standards and framework for the project. The sections in Table 2-1 depict the typical tasks involved in the solution architecture process within the wider context of the project lifecycle.

***Table 2-1.*** *Typical Tasks in The Solution Architecture Process*

| Project Phases | Solutions Architecture Activities |
| --- | --- |
| Initiation/problem definition | • Understand the business strategy<br>• Understand the business architecture<br>• Current state assessment (business/technology) |
| Requirements and analysis | • Identify business use cases<br>• Gather functional requirements<br>• Derive/gather non-functional requirements |
| Architecture and design | • Conduct POCs<br>• Finalize solution's technology stack<br>• Select a technical architectural framework<br>• Align with EA<br>• Create a high-level design/target technology architecture<br>• Assess technical risk<br>• Participate in the low-level design |
| Build/development | • Ensure deliverables are in line with the target technical architecture |
| Testing | |
| Deployment/ implementation | |
| Operations and maintenance | • Operational activities |

For the remainder of this book, I will categorize the activities carried out in the first two phases of the project lifecycle (Initiation/requirements and Analysis) as "**Fostering digital and business alignment.**" They are covered in Chapter 3. The activities in this area are crucial in properly capturing business and related requirements, which form the foundation for building the technical architecture of the digital solution and delivering the final product. Topics discussed in this chapter include understanding the business strategy and architecture, identifying business use cases, and gathering functional and non-functional requirements.

Activities listed under the project phase "Architecture and design" are categorized as "**Creating the target digital technology architecture**" and are covered in Chapter 4. It encompasses topics such as conducting proof of concepts, finalizing the solution's technology stack, aligning with EA, creating a high-level design or target technology architecture, and assessing technical risk. These activities form the basis for building and implementing the digital solution and delivering a successful outcome.

However, the aforementioned should not imply that a solutions architect's role is confined only to certain phases of the project lifecycle. The solutions architect also significantly contributes to the low-level design of the project, testing phases, and even plays a part in operational tasks. Let's delve into these roles briefly.

## The Solutions Architect's Responsibilities in Low-Level Design

The extent of the solutions architect's involvement in low-level design may vary depending on the size and complexity of the project and also based on the organization's requirements. In some cases, especially the low- to medium-complexity projects, a solutions architect may get heavily involved in the detailed design specifications for each component and subsystem of the solution. In other more complex projects, however, the solutions architect may delegate these tasks to other members of the design and development team. It is important to note that while solutions architects are responsible for guiding the development team in the implementation of the solution, they are not typically involved in the day-to-day low-level design or programming tasks. Instead, they work with the development team to provide guidance and ensure that the overall architecture of the solution is sound.

In cases where organizations define the role of a solutions architect at a much more technical level, the solutions architect works with developers to provide detailed design specifications for each component and subsystem in the solution. This includes defining interfaces between components, designing algorithms, selecting specific technologies and tools, and providing detailed technical specifications that guide the development team in their implementation efforts. In such cases, the solutions architect must ensure that the low-level design is consistent with the high-level design and meets all the requirements of the solution.

I should emphasize that while solutions architects may be involved in low-level design activities and programming tasks, these tasks are not typically part of their primary responsibilities. This is especially true in projects that are characterized by high complexity. These projects necessitate that solutions architects invest a significant portion of their time in strategic activities. This is because complex projects often involve numerous interconnected components, diverse technologies, and deal with intricate business processes. Consequently, the role of the solutions architect expands beyond just technical considerations. As you will observe in subsequent chapters, they need to devise a comprehensive strategy that accounts for both present requirements and future scalability. They must thoroughly understand the business domain, identify potential risks, ensure alignment with business goals, and plan for potential changes in the business or technology landscape. Moreover, these projects could require advanced technological capabilities such as distributed systems or microservices, high data processing needs, and robust security measures. These aspects add additional layers of complexity and necessitate strategic planning to ensure the system is scalable, secure, maintainable, and capable of meeting the business's needs. If a solutions architect is spending too much time on low-level design and programming types of activities, this can compromise their overall responsibility of integrating the different components of the solution. Therefore, in digital projects of high complexity, solutions architects often find themselves acting as a bridge between the technical teams and business stakeholders, facilitating communication and ensuring that the final solution aligns with both business objectives and technical constraints.

## Development and Testing Phases

Solutions architects bear a multitude of responsibilities spanning across the development and testing phases of the project lifecycle. During the development phase, they play a pivotal role in ensuring that the development team adheres to established technical standards and thoroughly meets both functional and non-functional requirements. They also act as crucial problem solvers, facilitating the resolution of any escalated technical issues, thereby bridging the gap between intricate technical aspects and project success. Moreover, they ensure that these technical issues are resolved according to best practices and industry standards.

Similarly, throughout the testing phase, the solutions architect collaborates with the testing team to ensure that the application undergoes rigorous testing and meets the quality and performance standards established during the design phase. They also assist in identifying and resolving any technical issues that might surface during testing.

In essence, solutions architects bear responsibilities in both the development and testing activities, primarily at a higher level. Their role is to ensure that the digital solution is architected, designed, developed, and tested to meet the requirements, standards, and expectations outlined in the project. This involves active participation across all project phases and a commitment to ensuring that the final product is of the highest quality.

# Operational Role of a Solutions Architect

Although solutions architects typically don't have an active role in the operational aspects of the digital solutions, they do have some responsibilities in ensuring that the delivered system run smoothly and effectively. Operational roles typically involve day-to-day management and maintenance of the implemented system, including monitoring, troubleshooting, and ensuring that the system operates efficiently and effectively. These roles are often performed by operations teams, IT administrators, or other technical staff who have a more hands-on role in the maintenance and management of the system.

Once the system has been implemented, the solutions architect's role usually shifts to one of oversight and guidance, ensuring that the implemented solution aligns with the original design and that it continues to meet the needs of the business. They may also provide guidance and recommendations on any future changes or enhancements that may be required.

Some of the responsibilities that solutions architects have in an operational setting may include the following:

- They monitor the system for a specified period of time to ensure that it performs adequately and that their design for the system satisfies business and technical requirements.

- They may note observations as lessons learned and use those insights towards architecting future solutions and systems.

- In cases where operational requirements change or special attention is needed for scalability, security, disaster recovery, or other areas, they may be called upon to provide guidance and recommendations.

Throughout this journey, the solutions architect plays a key role in ensuring that the overall solutions architecture remains aligned with the business requirements and objectives. They may also be involved in ongoing monitoring and performance analysis, identifying areas for improvement, and making recommendations to optimize the system's performance and efficiency.

## Key Solutions Architecture Deliverables

Throughout the solutions architecture process, the solutions architect produces several deliverables and contributes to many others. These deliverables are discussed in subsequent chapters. However, I should note that the primary deliverable of the solutions architecture process and activities is the solution's target technology architecture. It's also commonly referred to as the "solution design" document or blueprint that outlines the technical solution for a given business problem or opportunity. This document typically includes details and specifications of the hardware, software, network, and other technical components required to implement the solution. It also outlines the integration points between different components, the data flow, and the system's overall architecture.

The target architecture/solution design document serves as a guide for the development and implementation team and ensures that the solution meets the business requirements and operates as intended. The solutions architect ensures that the project's technical artifacts and other deliverables align with this target architecture, thereby contributing to the successful delivery of the solution.

# Solutions Architecture vs. Enterprise Architecture

In this section, I will discuss the solutions architecture domain within the context of enterprise architecture (EA). As mentioned, the solutions architecture of the project must align with the enterprise architecture to ensure that the digital solution is compatible with the overall business and digital/technology strategy of the organization. To begin, here's an overview of the enterprise architecture domain before delving into the distinctions between the two roles.

## The Enterprise Architecture Process

An organization can be viewed in terms of its business processes, the applications it uses to run its operations, the technologies it employs, and the data it generates and utilizes. Thus, the EA process involves creating a comprehensive view of the current and future state of the enterprise concerning its business processes, applications, overall technology landscape, and the underlying data required to support the organization's business strategy [4].

For instance, Sales and Finance are typical "business processes" of an organization, while CRM and e-commerce are examples of "applications" that support these processes. The software, hardware, and networking technologies used to facilitate these business processes constitute the "technology" dimension of the EA. Finally, customer data and order data are part of the data domain of the EA.

Consolidating information related to various dimensions in one place facilitates a comprehensive understanding of the interrelationships between these elements for an organization and its architects. This consolidation is where the value of EA becomes evident. For example, knowing which applications within an organization support its sales business processes can guide decision-making during the transformation of these processes. A comprehensive view of the enterprise also enables the organization to thoroughly understand its current architecture before making decisions about developing a new target architecture. This new architecture may include modifications to business processes, the introduction of new applications, and other changes.

Also, given that an EA may encompass a vast amount of information concerning an organization's business processes, applications, technologies, and data, each of these elements can involve a significant amount of complexity. As a result, these four elements are considered sub-architectures in their own right. Therefore, enterprise architecture consists of the business architecture, information architecture, applications architecture, and technology architecture.

Let's review each of the four dimensions in further detail.

The **business architecture** describes how an organization functions, and it includes information on the organization's strategy, governance, organization, and key business processes. This domain offers a comprehensive understanding of an organization's business by providing an overview of its business strategies, overall capabilities, business processes, products and services, assets, customers and stakeholders, and the underlying business rules that bind the organization together as a cohesive entity. Some of the topics related to business architecture include the following:

- The key business processes and functions within the organization

- The interaction and interrelation of these business processes

- The strategic goals and objectives of the organization

- The alignment of business functions with the organization's overall strategy

- The current business capabilities and the capabilities needed for future growth

- The ways technology can support and enhance business functions and processes

The **application architecture** within enterprise architecture outlines the strategy for managing the software applications in an organization. This domain provides a comprehensive view of the applications utilized by the organization, along with associated details such as the structure of the applications, technologies employed, development methodologies, integration strategies, various layers of applications and systems, and more. Discussions related to application architecture include the following:

- The structure of the new system or application, including its presentation, business, data, and other layers

- Various technologies utilized in building the application, such as monolithic, microservices-based, or cloud-native

- Technologies and methodologies for integrating the application components, including APIs, middleware, or message queues

- Scalability and performance strategies to handle increasing demand and ensure high availability

- Security measures at the data, application, and network levels to protect the application

- Supporting the organization's business processes and information flow within the application

- Managing changes, updates, patches, and new feature rollouts over time

- Post-deployment plans for application maintenance and support

- Alignment of application architecture with the broader enterprise architecture

- Data handling, storage, retrieval, and management strategies within the application

The **technology architecture** within enterprise architecture delineates the hardware, software technologies, and IT infrastructure of the business. This domain encompasses all the technology or infrastructure components of the organization, including network and hardware elements. It spans across areas related to the organization's network architecture, data center architecture, and hosting architecture, along with various infrastructure services, such as compute services and storage services.

The following topics and questions relate to this domain:

- Assessment of the current state of the organization's IT infrastructure, encompassing hardware, software, and network components

- The alignment of the existing technology infrastructure with the organization's business needs and objectives

- Plans for scaling the IT infrastructure to accommodate future growth and increased demand

- Integration strategies for incorporating new technologies into the existing infrastructure

- Measures in place to ensure the security and resilience of the IT infrastructure

- Ensuring data integrity, security, and privacy within the technology architecture

- Facilitation of data flow and information exchange across the organization through the technology architecture

- Strategy for managing and maintaining the IT infrastructure, including updates, upgrades, and problem resolution

The **information architecture** domain within enterprise architecture focuses on the structure and organization of information across the organization. It provides a comprehensive view of all the data and information within the organization by illustrating all data sources, storage methods, and various other aspects related to how that data is interconnected and managed. Information architecture offers a detailed view of both internal and external information within the organization, the various types of information, and how that information is stored, including in databases, data warehouses, data lakes, and files. Additionally, it outlines the diverse ways in which the information is processed and managed within the organization, taking into account elements such as information security, information quality, and other relevant aspects.

When discussing information architecture, the following topics are typically considered to be of high importance:

- Assessment of the current structure and organization of data and information within the organization

- Identification of data sources and understanding how data is collected, processed, and stored

- Evaluation of how the current state of information architecture aligns with the organization's business objectives and strategies

- Examination of protocols and technologies implemented for data security, privacy, and compliance with relevant regulations

- Ensuring data quality, accuracy, and integrity within the organization

- Ensuring information accessibility and usability across different business functions

- The flow of information between different business functions

- Strategies for managing and maintaining databases, data warehouses, data lakes, and other data storage systems

- Handling data integration across various systems and platforms within the organization

# The Difference Between Enterprise Architecture and Solutions Architecture

At the outset, although the activities that a solutions architect performs may seem similar to those carried out by the EA team, the main difference lies in the overall scope and level of detail. As discussed earlier, EA illustrates the current and target state of an enterprise, reflecting the overall business and technology capabilities of the organization. On the other hand, while solutions architecture also covers all four dimensions of EA, it has a more limited scope of coverage in each domain as it mainly focuses on the solution itself. Therefore, it is considered a subset of the overall EA. When developing a solutions architecture, the SA typically references the EA of the enterprise to obtain guidance on the technology strategy, standards, and best practices for implementing digital solutions, ensuring alignment with the organization's overall technology vision and goals. Figure 2-1 illustrates this difference.

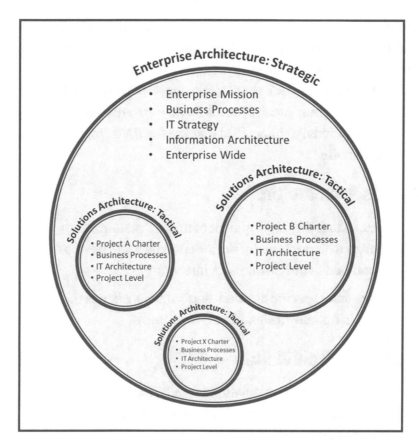

***Figure 2-1.*** *Scope of enterprise architecture vs. solutions architecture*

## Example: Difference Between Enterprise Architecture and Solutions Architecture

For example, suppose an organization decides to develop an IoT digital platform to support its IoT-based applications. In that case, the solutions architect would typically refer to the enterprise technology architecture to check if there is any previous guidance available on building such solutions in the enterprise. This guidance may provide the solutions architect with ideas on the organization's preferred technologies for IoT, standards that should be followed, best practices related to integrating IoT solutions with the rest of the enterprise, and so on.

To be more specific, let's consider the types of questions that a solutions architect may pose to the EA team. Here are some examples of questions a Solutions Architect (SA) may ask the EA team, related to each of the four domains:

# Business Architecture

- How does the development of this IoT platform align with our broader business strategy and goals as outlined in our business architecture?

- Are there specific business performance metrics that the IoT platform should help to improve?

# Information Architecture

- How should the IoT platform handle data privacy and security given our current enterprise information architecture guidelines?

- What specific data standards and formats should the IoT platform comply with to ensure seamless data integration?

# Technical Architecture

- Are there any specific protocols or technologies prescribed by our technical architecture for IoT communication?

- What are the specific scalability and performance requirements outlined by our enterprise technical architecture that the IoT platform needs to meet?

# Application Architecture

- What are the integration points and interoperability requirements with our existing application ecosystem?

- Are there any specific application patterns or architectural styles (like microservices) recommended by our enterprise application architecture for IoT solutions?

The above shows the importance of the SA working and collaborating closely with the EA team. Working closely with the EA team can provide the solutions architect with a better understanding of the overall enterprise environment, including the current state of the organization's technology landscape, its business processes, and its strategic goals. By having access to this information, the solutions architect can more effectively design and implement solutions that align with the organization's overall direction and goals.

In addition, close collaboration between the solutions architect and the EA team can help ensure consistency and adherence to enterprise-wide standards, such as security and compliance requirements, that might otherwise be overlooked if the solutions architect worked in isolation. By leveraging the expertise of the EA team, solutions architects can benefit from their knowledge of the organization's technology and business landscape and avoid any potential missteps or conflicts that could arise from working in silos.

Overall, a strong partnership between solutions architects and the EA team can lead to more efficient and effective solution design and implementation, and ultimately help the organization achieve its strategic goals.

# The Solutions Architect and the Other Architects in Organizations

Let's now focus on the role of a solutions architect and differentiate it from other architects who may potentially work on a digital solution. Depending on how an organization defines the role of a solutions architect, it's common to have multiple specialized "architect" roles on a project. The typical approach is for a solutions architect to lead other architects, such as an application architect or a database architect, among others. This is because the solutions architect is responsible for integrating all domains. By having specialized architects on the team, the project can benefit from their expertise in their respective areas, which ultimately leads to a more robust solution. For example, specialized architect roles may focus on domains such as Big Data, Apache Kafka, AWS, Azure, and others [5].

In projects with a smaller scope, a solutions architect may end up fulfilling various architectural roles, whereas larger projects may require dedicated architects depending on the scope of each technical sub-domain. This, again, depends on how an organization defines the role of a solutions architect, the actual project and its complexities, as well as the organization's internal policies [6].

Additionally, in projects where one type of activity is more dominant than the others, it is common to see specialist architects acting in the capacity of the solutions architect. For example, in projects where the majority of technical activity is related to software design and development, the software architect may also act as the solutions architect for the project.

The following provides more information about the other architects who are typically involved in projects.

**Software architect:** A software architect focuses on the software aspects of distributed applications. They are responsible for the architecture, design, development, testing, and deployment issues related to software applications. While software architecture is mainly concerned with the architecture of the software application, the solutions architecture definition is broader in nature, encompassing software, hardware, network, and other components required to create the overall solution.

**Infrastructure architect:** Their focus is on the infrastructure elements of the digital/cloud solution. They are responsible for activities related to designing, deploying, and maintaining instances, hardware, storage, compute, network, and various other data center-related equipment.

**Enterprise architect:** Due to the nature of their role and function, the EAs possess a high-level view of both the business and IT aspects of an organization. This role is primarily located in the EA department of the organization rather than being part of a digital solution project. Similar to solutions architects, enterprise architects have a good understanding of both business and technology domains.

**Business architect:** The focus of a business architect is typically on the business and its processes. For instance, a business architect in the financial industry may specialize in financial processes, while a business architect in the healthcare industry would concentrate on the business processes specific to healthcare.

**Data/Information architect:** A data architect primarily operates at the enterprise level, overseeing the information flow throughout the enterprise or solution. They offer a comprehensive view of data across applications and systems and assess its value to the enterprise. Data architects work on transforming operational data into insights, optimizing data security, and maximizing the overall value of data. It's important to note that this role should not be confused with that of a database architect.

**Database architect:** A database architect specializes in database technologies and is accountable for designing, implementing, and maintaining solution-specific data models and databases. In most cases, each digital or cloud solution employs a database architect to ensure the database requirements of the system are fulfilled.

**Application architect:** An application architect concentrates on the business applications of the organization and is accountable for designing, developing, testing, and implementing them. Their main focus is on researching and understanding the advantages and disadvantages of application-related technologies and determining how to use them effectively within the organization. Application architects who specialize in application design are also known as software architects.

**Network architect:** The primary responsibility of a network architect is to design and construct organizational networks, which encompasses a broad range of tasks. However, when it comes to building cloud solutions, the network architect's role may not be as significant because the solution's specific scope assumes the presence and operation of various underlying network capabilities. It's important to note that network architecture is a vast field that encompasses many aspects beyond just building cloud solutions.

**Security architect:** Similar to network architects, security architects have a broad scope within the organizational context. Their primary responsibility for a cloud solution is to ensure it aligns with the overall organizational security framework and doesn't expose any data or organizational assets to unauthorized access. The role of security architecture in cloud solutions is crucial to maintaining the security and integrity of organizational data and assets.

In conclusion, it's important to note that the role of specialized architects may vary during the lifecycle of a project, depending on its scope. This variability makes the task of the solutions architect more challenging because they must ensure that all activities of all architects in each phase are coordinated with business stakeholders, and the outputs of each of those activities are reconciled with other activities. The SA plays a crucial role in ensuring that all architectural components of the solution are integrated effectively and aligned with the business objectives of the project.

In summary, the role of a digital solutions architect is broad and encompasses all the above-discussed architectural roles. They collaborate with the various specialized architects to ensure that a solution aligns with the organization's business requirements.

# Tailoring the Solutions Architecture Process

As noted in earlier chapters, the solutions architecture process can vary from one digital solution to another due to differences in the requirements, goals, and constraints of each. For example, a digital solution that uses a legacy technology stack may have different considerations around scalability and performance compared to a modern system that uses cloud-native technologies. Similarly, a system that is designed for a small user base may have different security and privacy requirements compared to a system that is designed for a large user base.

While the high-level steps of the solutions architecture process are typically the same, the details and specific considerations could also vary based on the system and technology stack being used. For example, the evaluation of technology options and the selection of a technology stack may be more complex for a system that requires high scalability and performance compared to a system with simpler requirements. Similarly, the design of the system's security and privacy features may require different approaches depending on the technology stack being used.

As architects transition from one project to another, they must be aware of the specific context and requirements of each project and make necessary adjustments to their approach, methodology, and techniques. The level of modifications required will vary depending on factors such as project size, complexity, and technology stack. Therefore, they must tailor their approach to suit the overall scope of the project.

Architects must consider several factors when transitioning from one project to another. The following are some examples of these factors, which will be elaborated further in later parts of the book:

- **Understanding the business context:** Architects need to understand the business context of each project, including its goals, objectives, and constraints. This helps them align their architecture vision and design with the business needs of the project.

- **Adapting the methodology:** The methodology used in one project may not be suitable for another project due to differences in the size, complexity, and team structure. Therefore, architects need to adapt their methodology to fit the specific context of the project. For example, they may need to adopt an agile methodology for a project that requires fast iterations and frequent feedback.

- **Customizing the architecture approach:** Architects need to customize their architecture approach to fit the specific requirements of each project. For example, they may need to focus more on performance and scalability in a project that handles large volumes of data or traffic.

- **Adapting to the technology stack:** Different technology stacks require different approaches to architecture design. For example, a project using a legacy technology stack may require a different architecture design than a project using modern cloud-native technologies.

- **Adjusting communication and collaboration:** The communication and collaboration practices that worked in one project may not be suitable for another project. Therefore, architects need to adjust their communication and collaboration practices to fit the specific context of each project. For example, they may need to use different communication channels or tools to collaborate with team members.

# Example

Let's illustrate this by an example. The steps involved in building an AI/ML system may be different than building an IoT solution for a manufacturing facility due to differences in the underlying technology, data sources, and business goals. In building an AI/ML system, the key steps include identifying the problem to be solved, preparing and cleaning the data, selecting and training the appropriate machine learning models, and evaluating the performance of the models. This involves a strong focus on data quality, feature engineering, and model selection to ensure accurate predictions and insights.

In contrast, building an IoT solution for a manufacturing facility involves identifying the key sensors and data sources, setting up the necessary infrastructure and connectivity, and developing the appropriate analytics and control algorithms. This involves a strong focus on real-time data processing, edge computing, and network optimization to ensure reliable and efficient data collection and analysis.

Additionally, the business goals of an AI/ML system and an IoT solution for a manufacturing facility may be different. The primary goal of an AI/ML system is to generate insights and predictions that can be used to improve business outcomes such as customer satisfaction, revenue growth, or operational efficiency. In contrast, the primary goal of an IoT solution for a manufacturing facility is to optimize the production process, reduce downtime, and improve safety and quality.

Overall, while there may be some similarities in the steps involved in building an AI/ML system and an IoT solution for a manufacturing facility, there are also key differences in the technology, data sources, and business goals that require a tailored approach for each solution. Architects, therefore, need to be adaptable and flexible as they move from one project to another. They need to be able to understand the specific context and requirements of each project and make necessary changes to their approach, methodology, and techniques to ensure that the architecture design meets the needs of the project.

# Summary

This chapter provided you with an overview of the solutions architecture domain and its importance in ensuring that digital solutions align with an organization's broader strategic goals and architectural principles. The chapter discussed the process, activities, and integration of solutions architecture within the project lifecycle and the organization's enterprise architecture process. By understanding the role of solutions architecture in a project, you now have insights into how it contributes to achieving project objectives and how it integrates with other project activities. The chapter also covered the distinction between solutions architecture and enterprise architecture, the role of the solutions architect, and how the solutions architecture process can be tailored to suit a project's specific needs.

Overall, the chapter aimed to provide you with a clear understanding of the solutions architecture domain and its importance in achieving successful digital solutions. By providing insights into the process, activities, and integration of solutions architecture within the broader context of a project and organization's EA process, you can gain a better understanding of how solutions architecture fits into the overall plan and how it contributes to achieving project objectives.

# References

1. The Open Group. (2011). *The Open Group Architecture Framework (TOGAF) Version 9.1*. Chapter 3: Architecture Content Framework. Retrieved March 2, 2023, from `https://pubs.opengroup.org/architecture/togaf91-doc/arch/chap03.html#tag_03_65`

2. Gartner. (n.d.). "Solution Architecture. IT Glossary." Retrieved March 2, 2023, from `www.gartner.com/en/information-technology/glossary/solution-architecture`

3. Stack Overflow. (n.d.). "Software design vs software architecture." Retrieved March 27, 2023, from `https://stackoverflow.com/questions/704855/software-design-vs-software-architecture`

4. Government Accountability Office. (2001). "Information Technology Investment Management: A Framework for Assessing and Improving Process Maturity (Exposure Draft)." Retrieved March 27, 2023, from `www.gao.gov/assets/a77237.html`

5. Lam, M. (August 7, 2008). "What is a solutions architect? A vital role for IT-business alignment." *CIO*. Retrieved March 6, 2023, from `www.cio.com/article/191394/what-is-a-solutions-architect-a-vital-role-for-it-business-alignment.html`

6. Briq, I. (March 17, 2019). "The Software Architecture Roles." *Medium*. Retrieved March 27, 2023, from `https://medium.com/@briqi/the-software-architecture-roles-3bfccc9e36d2`

# CHAPTER 3

# Fostering Digital and Business Alignment

In this chapter, I will discuss the importance of business alignment, its benefits, and how solutions architecture can help achieve it. I will also explore the key considerations and best practices for solutions architects to design and deliver digital solutions that meet the business needs and align with the overall organizational goals.

Business alignment is the process of ensuring that an organization's various activities and processes are aligned with its business strategies, goals, and objectives. It involves making sure that different aspects of the organization work together to support and reinforce the overall operations of the business.

While the concept of business alignment should apply to all aspects of an organization and its businesses, historically it has been used more in technology circles to ensure that an organization's technology investments and related initiatives are aligned with the highest level of business strategies, goals, and objectives. Without proper alignment, digital solutions may not meet organizational goals, resulting in wasted time, resources, and money. A lack of business alignment can also lead to poor user adoption, system performance, and ultimately, project failure. Therefore, ensuring business alignment is essential for the success of any digital solutions project.

© Wasim Rajput 2023
W. Rajput, *Solutions Architecture*, https://doi.org/10.1007/978-1-4842-9657-8_3

# Example: Misalignment of Technology and Business

Suppose an organization wants to implement an AI-based solution to enhance its customer service. The company has a high volume of customer inquiries and a limited number of support staff, leading to the decision to invest in an AI chatbot. The hope is that this chatbot will reduce wait times, operate around the clock, and efficiently resolve customer queries. This chatbot is trained using previous customer service interactions and is integrated into the company's website and mobile app.

However, let's imagine that post-deployment, the chatbot fails to meet these expectations. The chatbot often misunderstands complex customer queries and provides unrelated responses, leading to customer frustration. Its problem-solving capabilities is limited to standard issues, and it struggles with unique problems or complaints that require the nuanced understanding of a human agent. Moreover, the chatbot is unable to offer personalized responses or recommendations based on customer history or preferences, a key aspect of customer satisfaction in the company's service ethos. The result is a significant drop in customer satisfaction scores.

This example represents a situation where a digital project implementation doesn't align with the business's needs and objectives, leading to adverse outcomes rather than the intended benefits.

A solutions architect, therefore, must take proactive steps to ensure that the delivered solutions are aligned with the business's strategies and objectives. Among other things, this involves understanding the business context in which solutions are being developed, understanding the business priorities, translating them into technical requirements, and designing solutions that address both the technical and business needs. By doing so, the solutions architect ensures that the digital solutions delivered to the organization are aligned with the organization's overall business goals, resulting in increased user adoption, improved system performance, and successful project outcomes.

# The Solutions Architect's Role in Business Alignment

Aligning digital solutions with business strategies requires alignment at all levels of the organization. From CIOs aligning their highest-level technology strategies with an organization's business executives and programmers delivering specific functionality to the business users, processes and practices should be in place to maximize alignment at all levels of the organization.

As the senior technical person responsible for designing and delivering digital solutions, the solutions architect plays a vital role in ensuring alignment with the organization's objectives and goals.

To ensure that alignment, solutions architects perform several functions including:

- Acting as a liaison between the business and technology teams, discussing broader project concerns with business executives, and sometimes explaining technical details as well. For example, this could mean discussing the scope and goals of a new CRM implementation with business executives and also distilling complex technical aspects of the system into comprehensible terms.

- Maintaining a strong relationship with the business stakeholders throughout the duration of the project and after its successful delivery. For example, after the launch of a new e-commerce platform, a solutions architect might continue to collaborate with the marketing team, refining features based on user feedback and market trends.

- Constantly communicating technology-related issues to the business team and keeping them informed about the relevance of technology to the business problem. Solutions architects explain technology in clear business terms, making it understandable for business users. Suppose during the development of a new cloud-based data analytics platform, there are potential delays due to unforeseen technical challenges. The solutions architect would communicate this to the business team, explaining the issue and its implications in clear business terms.

- Ensuring that the solution's architecture remains aligned with the organization's business strategy at all levels, including building new technologies, defining new processes, and building data repositories.

By taking on these roles, solutions architects can ensure that technology investments and initiatives align with the organization's business strategies, goals, and objectives. I will elaborate on the specific set of activities and processes required for alignment in subsequent sections of this chapter. I will focus on diverse strategies and best practices that can enhance this alignment to its maximum potential.

# Using Business Strategy to Drive Solutions Architecture

One of the common reasons for the subpar performance of digital transformation projects is the technical team's incomplete understanding of the overall business context. This lack of understanding can lead to a misalignment between the technological solutions being implemented and the actual needs of the business [1]. It can also prevent the solutions architect from recommending better and more innovative solutions to the business. By gaining a better understanding of the organization's goals, processes, and systems, as well as industry and market trends, solutions architects can design and implement more effective digital solutions that align with the overall strategy and objectives of the business.

Let's illustrate this with a simple example. Suppose a software development team is tasked with building a new customer relationship management (CRM) system for a retail business. If they do not understand the business strategy of the retail company, they may not design the CRM system to meet the specific needs of the business. This can lead to inefficiencies in the system, such as irrelevant or redundant features, that could negatively impact the user experience and customer satisfaction.

For instance, if the retail company's business strategy is focused on providing a highly personalized shopping experience, the CRM system should be designed to gather and analyze customer data to provide tailored recommendations and offers. If the development team does not understand this business strategy, they may create a generic CRM system that does not account for the need for personalization. This can result in lower customer engagement and decreased sales.

A solutions architect, therefore, should start the process of attaining a better understanding of the business context by first gaining insight into its strategy. A business strategy is a long-term plan and direction a company or a LOB (Line of Business) follows to achieve its objectives and goals. Besides highlighting an organization's goals and objectives, the plan also highlights the critical steps and programs needed to compete in the market, provide value to customers, create new markets, and create a plan to become profitable and sustain profits over an extended period of time. The strategy also provides insights on the organization's decisions related to resource allocation, product and service development, target market selection, customer acquisition, and risk management.

By understanding an organization's business strategy, a solutions architect can gather business requirements for the solution they are working on in a more strategic way. This can also enable them to recommend technical solutions that are more aligned with the organization's goals and offer more strategic benefits to the organization. Understanding the business strategy and overall business architecture (which will be explained later in this chapter) puts both the solutions architect and the business stakeholders in lockstep towards achieving the ultimate objectives of delivering the best products and services, providing high customer value, and doing so at the lowest possible cost [2].

# The Intersection of Business Strategy and Solutions Architecture: Essential Dimensions and Components

Let's now review how the various components of a business strategy [3] can help solutions architects gain a better understanding of the organization's goals and objectives. Figure 3-1 illustrates this recommended alignment.

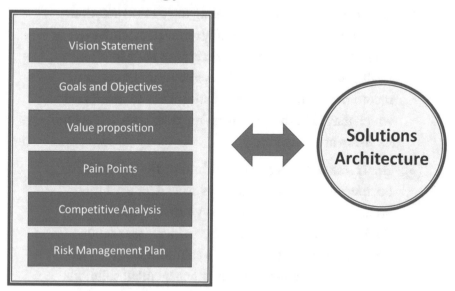

**Business Strategy**

*Figure 3-1.* *Alignment of a digital solution's architecture with an organization's business strategy*

- **Vision statement:** The vision statement outlines the company's vision for the future. This information can help solutions architects understand the company's aspirations and can accordingly help them recommend more strategic solutions to their business customers. Consider a scenario where a business aims to reduce its carbon emissions by 50% in the long term. Although this objective may not be directly related to the solution requirements that a solutions architect is working on, being aware of it can enable the solutions architect to recommend a more strategic analytics solution. This solution can help the organization track its carbon emissions and make data-driven decisions that accelerate the achievement of its long-term vision, instead of merely meeting the tactical solution requirements that were initially requested. Similarly, if a healthcare provider's vision is to provide free healthcare to its patients, the solutions architect can recommend a telemedicine platform at a reduced cost, which may help the healthcare provider with achieving its vision at a better cost.

- **Goals and objectives:** Understanding the broader business goals and objectives is crucial for a solutions architect to align their solution with those goals. For instance, if a company aims to increase revenue within a specified timeframe, a solutions architect may propose better online customer engagement solutions, which can not only enhance customer engagement but also accelerate revenue growth in a shorter period, aligning with the business's overall objectives.

- **Value proposition:** The value proposition outlines the unique value that the company offers to its customers. Understanding this value proposition can help solutions architects design technological solutions that enhance the company's unique value proposition and support the company's competitive advantage. For instance, let's consider the healthcare provider example mentioned earlier. Suppose its value proposition is centered around offering personalized healthcare services. Knowing this can enable a solutions architect to recommend an improved business analytics and BI (Business Intelligence) solution, which can help identify patterns and specific conditions in patients. This can enable the healthcare provider to offer personalized care options and forecast situations for better patient care.

- **Pain points:** When describing new goals and objectives, a business strategy document can highlight the organization's earlier pain points that motivated them to pursue a new direction. By understanding these pain points, solutions architects can gain valuable insights into the organization's challenges and envision solutions that not only address these pain points but also prevent their recurrence. For example, a retail company may attribute its sluggish sales to an inefficient sales process. An analysis of the process and its related systems may drive the solutions architect to recommend a digital platform and supporting processes that can address the various inefficiencies in the old process.

- **Competitive analysis:** A competitive analysis provides insights into the company's competition and their strengths and weaknesses. A solutions architect's deeper understanding of new technologies and related trends can help them recommend better solutions. For instance, by understanding the technical underpinnings of ChatGPT, a cutting-edge software that employs advanced natural language processing (NLP) techniques, deep neural networks, language modeling, and machine learning algorithms, solutions architects can suggest utilizing similar technologies to develop state of the art chatbots to interact with their clients.

- **Risk management plan:** The risk management plan, often developed in conjunction with an organization's business strategy, is designed to identify potential risks that could negatively impact the company's success.

It also includes relevant risk mitigation strategies to reduce the likelihood or impact of those risks, as well as contingency plans to address them should they occur. Understanding this information can help solutions architects design technology solutions that mitigate those risks form a technical perspective. For example, if the business's risk management plan identifies reputational risks as a major concern, the architect may recommend an online solution that extracts data from social media and include features to monitor and manage the business's online reputation.

In summary, understanding an organization's business strategy can provide solutions architects with a comprehensive view of the company's overall business environment. This, in turn, allows architects to devise more effective solutions that align with the organization's goals and objectives.

# Aligning Solutions Architecture with Business Architecture

In order to ensure maximum alignment with the business, solutions architects must also have a thorough understanding of an organization's business architecture. While the business strategy of a company provides solutions architects with an overview of the direction of an organization or a LOB, an organization's business architecture [4] can help solutions architects understand the following:

- The organization's **products and services** and how they, along with their supporting business processes and systems, will interact with the new digital solution

- The key **business processes** impacted by the digital business solution being architected and designed

- **Data and information** related to the organization's business processes

- **Business rules** related to the organization's business processes

- An organization's key **stakeholders** related to the various business processes

- Business **performance metrics**

- A visual representation of an **organization's capabilities**

The following elaborates further on the above. It is also summarized in Figure 3-2.

## Business Architecture

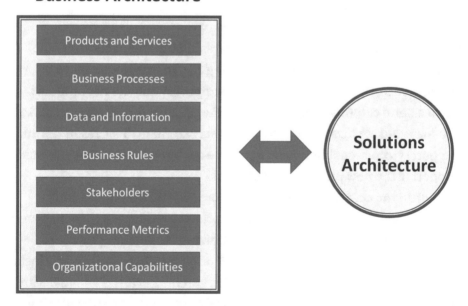

*Figure 3-2.*  *Alignment of a digital solution's architecture with an organization's business architecture*

# Products and Services

To ensure that digital solutions align with an organization's business needs, solutions architects should gain a broad understanding of the organization's products and services. Knowing the various products and services of the organizations and how they are delivered and supported can especially help solutions architects leverage existing organizational capabilities, especially if their solution is a new product or service. It can also help solutions architects with an understanding of the current operational support system and production environment related to existing products and services.

Having a clear understanding of the existing products, services, and the larger ecosystem surrounding them is also crucial for solutions architects because that knowledge can assist the architects in learning whether their solution requires integration with other products, services, or systems within the same ecosystem.

For example, if other products and services are supported by an organization's strategic ERP systems, the solutions architect can ensure that the solutions that they are developing also interface with those systems. Also, by leveraging the overall support system for the products, services, and resources that are used in the organization to support those products and services, a solutions architect can share those resources and support systems, enabling them to reduce costs related to the operational support of the new products and services.

Furthermore, acquiring in-depth knowledge of an organization's products and services plus the creation process and support mechanisms can assist the solutions architect in optimizing the support processes related to their solutions. For instance, if other products and services incur substantial operational costs, the solutions architect can collaborate with the operations teams to automate the operational processes concerning their solution. This would lead to enhanced operational efficiency and cost savings for the organization.

In summary, by getting an overview of an organization's products and services, as well as the support and operational ecosystem, a solutions architect can make informed decisions about whether their solution needs to be integrated with that ecosystem or if alternate strategies are needed to support their solutions or products and services when they are deployed in production.

# Business Processes

Business processes and value streams are another critical component of a business architecture. These are a series of tasks, activities, and flows that a business uses to deliver value to its customers. Learning this information can help the solutions architect to better understand the business requirements needed to serve an organization's business processes or in other cases to help it redesign those business processes. In fact, learning the details of business processes that may get impacted due to the new digital solution can help the technology team build innovative solutions to mitigate the impact.

For example, consider the case of a retail company that wants to implement a new e-commerce platform. As part of the work, the solutions architect needs to understand the company's business processes and value streams to ensure that the new platform will meet its needs. The architect may work with the company's business analysts to map out the different processes and activities involved in selling products online, including managing inventory and order fulfillment, handling payments, and customer service. By understanding these processes in detail, the architect can identify areas where the new platform can improve efficiency, reduce costs, or enhance the customer experience. They may suggest integrating the platform with the company's inventory management system to ensure that products are always in stock, or incorporating chatbots or other AI technologies to improve customer service. In this way, understanding the business processes and value streams is essential for developing effective solutions that meet the company's needs and deliver value to its customers.

An organization's business processes are usually reflected in a business process map. It typically consists of a series of process diagrams or flowcharts that show the steps involved in each process, including data flows, decision points, systems used, and other inputs and outputs. These process diagrams may relate to key processes such as sales, marketing, procurement, customer service and support, finance, operations, and HR, as well as supporting processes such as procurement, inventory management, and IT management. A solutions architect can request this document from the business to help them with their understanding of an organization's business processes.

# Data and Information Related to Business Processes

Data and information related to the various processes of the business are also an essential aspect of the business architecture. This includes understanding the different types of data that the business processes use, such as master data, transactional data, data quality attributes, and various data used for analytics. Master data is the core data that is essential to the business's operations, such as customer data, product data, and vendor data. Transactional data is the data that is generated during the execution of business processes, such as sales orders, invoices, and purchase orders. Data quality attributes refer to the characteristics of data that determine its accuracy, completeness, and consistency. In addition to these types of data, a business may also use various data for analytics, such as customer behavior data, market trend data, and financial data. Understanding the different types of data used by the business processes can help the solutions architect identify opportunities to improve data quality, automate data processing, and enable more effective analytics.

# Business Rules

Another critical piece of information that can be derived from a business architecture are the specific business rules related to the organization's business processes. These business rules govern the behavior and decision-making of various systems and stakeholders within the organization. Examples of business rules may include approval rules related to various processes and workflows, calculations performed in various processes, escalation rules, data validation rules, and more. By understanding these business rules, a solutions architect can design digital solutions that align with the organization's existing business practices and support compliance with regulatory requirements. For example, if the organization has a specific approval process for new product development, the solutions architect can design a solution that automates the approval process and integrates it with other systems. This can help ensure that new products are developed in a timely and compliant manner.

# An Organization's Stakeholders

One critical piece of information that a solutions architect should compile is that of the stakeholders who will be directly or indirectly associated with the solution. Knowledge of an organization's products and services, as well as its business processes, can help solutions architects gain a deeper understanding of key stakeholders. This understanding can broaden the architect's perspective when speaking to stakeholders for requirements gathering and other purposes. To gain a better understanding of stakeholders, a solutions architect should review the overall organizational structure, including stakeholder roles, business locations, channels used, and more. This information can help the solutions architect throughout the process of envisioning and designing the right solutions, as well as in ensuring that they cover all bases when gathering solution requirements.

# Business Performance Metrics

In addition to requesting visual representations and maps of the organization's business processes and workflows, a solutions architect should also request performance metrics that the business may be using to measure the efficiency and effectiveness of their processes. These performance metrics may include measures such as cycle time, cost per unit, defect rate, customer satisfaction, and employee productivity. By understanding these metrics, the solutions architect can gain a better understanding of the business's goals and objectives, as well as any pain points or areas of inefficiency. This information can help the architect identify areas where digital solutions can have the most significant impact and prioritize development efforts accordingly. Moreover, by understanding the performance metrics, the solutions architect can design digital solutions that address specific business needs and goals. For example, if the business's primary goal is to improve cycle time, the solutions architect may design a solution that automates manual processes or eliminates bottlenecks.

# Business Capabilities

An organization's business capabilities are another essential component of its business architecture. Understanding an organization's current capabilities can enable all stakeholders to make better decisions, prioritize future investment decisions, assess risks related to new initiatives, support an organization's transformation efforts, and encourage collaboration among stakeholders. Ultimately, it can help in the planning and building of new capabilities for the business.

An organization's business capabilities are usually reflected in a business capability map. It is a hierarchical visual representation of an organization's capabilities that shows how they relate to each other, with higher-level capabilities representing broader goals and objectives and lower-level capabilities representing specific functions and activities [5]. Having a business capability map of a LOB (line of business) can be extremely helpful for a solutions architect in several ways:

- **Understanding business requirements:** The business capability map can offer a lucid context for comprehending the business requirements and priorities of the LOB. This understanding assists the solutions architect in aligning their proposed solution with these capabilities.

- **Identifying opportunities for improvement:** The capability map can help identify opportunities for improvement or innovation in the LOB. This can be useful for the solutions architect in proposing new solutions that can enhance the LOB's capabilities and competitiveness.

- **Defining solution scope:** The capability map provides a clear picture of the LOB's capabilities and how they relate to each other. This helps the solutions architect define the scope of their proposed solution and ensure that it addresses all the necessary capabilities.

- **Communicating with stakeholders:** The capability map provides a common language and framework for communicating with stakeholders. This helps the solutions architect explain their proposed solutions in a way that is easily understandable and relevant to the LOB's business objectives.

In summary, having the business architecture of the organization that the solutions architect is building the digital solution for provides not only a framework to gather business requirements but also offers a complete picture of the context, ecosystem, and environment in which the digital solution will function. This helps the solutions architect in devising more strategic, aligned, and intelligent solutions. As observed, an organization's business architecture is a comprehensive framework that includes its products, services, key business processes, related data and rules, and key stakeholders. It details how these elements interact with new digital solutions, illustrating this interplay visually. It also defines the performance metrics to track success and visually represents the organization's capabilities. This architecture, therefore, serves as the foundation for aligning technology solutions with business goals.

# The Importance of Business Use Cases in Solutions Architecture

Business use cases are used in the solutions architecture process to identify and define specific business requirements and functionality. Solutions architects can use business use cases to understand business processes, user needs, and system requirements, and to develop a comprehensive understanding of how different systems and technologies will interact with each other. This helps solutions architects design and implement effective and efficient solutions that meet business needs, improve business processes, and create value for the organization.

A business use case describes how a particular system or technology is used to achieve the overall objectives of a specific business process, value stream, or the organization as a whole [6]. It outlines the actors and users involved in the business process, the information used, the process flow, and the inputs and outputs of the business use case. Essentially, a use case provides detailed insights into the users of the solution, the significance of the solution to the organization's business processes, and how the solution will interface with other systems to meet the user's requirements.

Business use cases can also serve as a starting point for further gathering of business requirements. When working with business stakeholders to discuss the various aspects of a business use case, solutions architects can get a comprehensive view of the business use case and identify other business processes that interact with it. This understanding can help solutions architects ensure that the integration with all secondary processes is seamless and meets the needs of the organization.

In addition to its use in the solutions architecture process, business use cases can serve as a tool for communicating with stakeholders about the intended functionality and benefits of the proposed solution. By presenting a clear and detailed picture of the solution's capabilities and benefits, business use cases can help facilitate stakeholder buy-in and support for the solution.

## Business Use Cases vs. Business Processes

It is important to distinguish between a business use case and a business process [7]. A business process refers to a broader perspective of a series of activities performed by both systems and individuals to achieve a specific business objective. It encompasses the end-to-end flow of operations and involves multiple steps and stakeholders. For example, the process of order fulfillment in organizations involves activities like order placement, order processing, inventory management, shipping, delivery, and more. It represents the overall structure and sequence of actions required to accomplish a particular goal.

On the other hand, a business use case focuses on a specific scenario or situation in which a particular system, technology, or approach is applied to address a specific business need or problem. It highlights the interaction between users, systems, and processes to achieve a desired outcome. For instance, when it comes to inventory management, automating inventory tracking or utilizing analytics to forecast demand are examples of business use cases. Automating inventory tracking involves implementing a system that continuously monitors stock levels and provides real-time visibility, while utilizing analytics to forecast demand helps optimize inventory levels and improve decision-making.

In summary, while a business process provides a comprehensive view of the overall sequence of activities, a business use case highlights a specific application or scenario that demonstrates how a particular approach or technology can be employed to address a specific business requirement.

# Business Use Cases vs. Business Requirements

Business use cases should also not be confused with detailed business requirements. While use cases describe the functional requirements of a system from the perspective of its users or stakeholders, detailed business requirements provide a more granular view of the specific features and functionality. It's important to understand the difference between these two concepts to ensure that the right information is captured and communicated to the development team.

Let's take the example of customer order placement on an online shopping platform. The use case describes the steps a customer takes to place an order for a product. It involves browsing the product catalog, adding items to the shopping cart, providing shipping and payment information, confirming the order, and receiving an order confirmation. This use case provides an overview of the customer's interaction with the system to complete a purchase.

To translate this use case into detailed business requirements, let's consider requirements for the payment options provided on the platform. The system should support multiple methods to provide customers with flexibility. Detailed business requirements would specify accepting credit card payments, PayPal payments, and payments through a third-party payment gateway. This ensures that customers can choose the payment method that suits them best.

By defining these detailed business requirements, the development team receives clear instructions on implementing the payment options and order confirmation functionalities. This level of specificity ensures that the system meets the business needs and provides a smooth and satisfactory customer experience.

# Business Use Case Examples

To ensure clarity, here are additional examples of business use cases:

- An organization may decide to build a BI and data analytics platform for its marketing department. The specific use cases in this case would be the identification of target audiences and personalization of marketing messages for better engagement and conversion rates.

- A business may decide to use chatbots and AI-powered tools to provide quick and personalized support to customers, reducing response times and increasing customer satisfaction. Getting customer feedback to help improve an organization's products or services would be a potential use case for these technologies.

- An organization may decide to implement SaaS-based contract management software with advanced analytics features. Tracking and managing legal agreements, reducing risk, and ensuring compliance would be the potential use cases for this example.

- A healthcare provider can use IoT technologies to monitor patients' health remotely, collecting real-time data on vital signs and other health indicators. The use case would be to use the data for analysis by healthcare professionals to detect potential health issues and provide timely interventions.

# Business Use Cases for New Technologies

Business use cases are also an important tool when considering the potential use of new technologies for an organization's business. For example, an organization that wants to consider the use of 5G technology in its manufacturing facilities due to its low latency and advanced IoT features can identify the following use cases for potential implementation:

- **Remote asset management:** With 5G, manufacturers can remotely monitor and manage assets in real time, reducing downtime and maintenance costs.

- **Augmented reality:** 5G can enable the use of augmented reality (AR) in manufacturing, allowing workers to see and interact with digital information overlaid onto their physical environment.

- **Quality control and inspection automation:** With 5G, manufacturers can automate quality control and inspection processes, ensuring high product standards and reducing errors.

- **Remote equipment monitoring and maintenance:** Leveraging 5G, manufacturers can remotely monitor and maintain equipment in real time, minimizing downtime and maintenance costs.

Here are other examples of business use cases in the context of applying new digital technologies:

- To optimize crop yield and reduce waste, IoT can be used to monitor environmental factors such as soil moisture, temperature, and humidity.

- The pharmaceutical industry is exploring the use of quantum computing to simulate molecular interactions, enabling scientists to identify new drug candidates more quickly and accurately. This could lead to the development of effective treatments for incurable diseases.

- To develop more sophisticated AI/ML models, quantum computing is being utilized to train them faster.

- Organizations considering the use of 5G technologies due to its low latency and advanced IoT features could consider its use for a number of use cases. For instance, remote asset management can be performed by manufacturers to monitor and manage assets in real time, reducing downtime and maintenance costs. Additionally, 5G can be used in augmented reality in manufacturing to allow workers to see and interact with digital information overlaid onto their physical environment.

- And many more

In conclusion, it is evident that understanding the distinction between business processes and business use cases is crucial when collecting business requirements at the appropriate level of detail. Failing to grasp this distinction can lead to a haphazard or unclear approach, resulting in the omission of vital details. This misalignment between the technology solutions being developed and the overarching business objectives can have detrimental effects on the effectiveness and efficiency of the final solution. Therefore, a meticulous approach to collecting business requirements, with a clear understanding of the difference between business processes and business use cases, is essential for achieving successful technology implementation and realizing the intended business benefits.

# Gathering Solution Requirements

After agreeing on the implementation of a particular use case, the business stakeholders and solutions architect can proceed to discuss the detailed business requirements related to it. These requirements provide a more detailed description of the specific features, functions, and behaviors that are required to support each business use case. They describe the specific inputs, outputs, and processing rules that must be implemented to support the business process or use case; they are typically documented in a structured format, such as a spreadsheet or database, to guide the development of the system.

During the process of gathering requirements, the solutions architect analyzes each requirement for feasibility and defines them in sufficient detail to ensure understanding by all project stakeholders. Throughout this process, the solutions architect also collaborates with the project manager to ensure that the defined business requirements stay within the defined project scope. This is important because, during the requirement gathering process, business users and stakeholders may add more requirements to the list, and the solutions architect's role is to ensure that the project scope remains under control.

When defining business requirements, it is important to identify both the functional and non-functional requirements of the project. Functional requirements describe the specific features, capabilities, and behaviors that the system must perform to meet the business needs. These requirements are typically related to specific business processes, use cases, or user stories (high-level description of use cases). They define what the system must do to satisfy the business requirements.

Non-functional requirements, on the other hand, describe the characteristics of the system that are not related to its specific functionality, but are important for its overall performance and usability. These requirements may include performance, scalability, reliability, security, usability, and other factors that are critical to the success of the project.

Let's explore both in further detail.

# Gathering Functional Requirements

Functional requirements are specifications that define the system's or digital solution's functionality from a user perspective. They are described in an easy-to-understand language by business users and may refer to business process flows or other functions that the system must fulfill. For instance, a functional requirement could be to develop machine learning algorithms for optimizing marketing campaigns. Another example could be to generate graphical representations of data and insights using visualization tools like PowerBI.

## Example: Functional Requirements of an AR Use Case

For example, let's consider the business use case of offering "augmented reality applications to users." AR is a technology that enhances real-world environments by overlaying digital information or virtual objects onto them, creating an immersive and interactive experience. AR is typically experienced through devices such as smartphones, tablets, or wearable headsets that use a camera and sensors to detect the user's environment and position digital objects within it. Furniture stores, for example, can enable their customers to see how their furniture would look in their home before making a purchase.

If we break that use case further down, some of the functional requirements for that use case could include the following:

- Customers should be able to access the AR application through their mobile device.

- The AR application should be able to superimpose images of furniture onto the camera view of the customer's home.

- The AR application should allow the customer to interact with the furniture images, such as changing their position or orientation.

- The application should integrate with external data and content using APIs.

## The Process of Gathering Functional Requirements

Here are some steps that solutions architects could take when gathering functional requirements of digital solutions.

1. **Identify all stakeholders:** It is crucial to identify all stakeholders involved in the implementation of digital solutions. The scope of such solutions can be extensive, and some stakeholders may not be immediately apparent. This is particularly relevant when new digital solutions need to integrate with an organization's existing legacy systems. For example, the stakeholders involved in implementing a new digital marketing campaign could include the marketing team, IT department, legal team, and third-party vendors. It is important to involve all relevant stakeholders in the planning and implementation stages to ensure successful adoption and integration of the solution.

2. **Conduct interviews:** It is recommended to conduct interviews with all stakeholders involved in the implementation of digital solutions, depending on the scope of the applications and systems. The interviews should aim to gather information on their requirements, concerns, and expectations for the solution. By doing so, it helps to ensure that the solution addresses the needs of all stakeholders and that potential issues are addressed early in the process. Additionally, the interviews can provide insights into any potential roadblocks that may arise during the implementation, which can be addressed before they become major obstacles.

3. **Create a functional requirements document:** Once the interviews are conducted, it is crucial to create a comprehensive functional requirements document that outlines all the necessary functionalities of the digital solution. The document should be created with inputs from all relevant stakeholders to ensure that it accurately reflects their requirements. The functional requirements document should include details such as the system's objectives, scope, and constraints, as well as a description of the system's main features and functions. It should also specify any technical requirements, performance criteria, and user interface specifications.

4. **Share the functional requirements document widely:** Once the functional requirements document is created, it should be shared widely among all stakeholders to ensure that everyone is on

the same page. The document can also be used as a basis for further discussions and to revalidate the requirements throughout the development process. Any changes made to the functional requirements should be documented and communicated to all stakeholders to ensure everyone is aware of the changes.

5. **Put the document under change control:** The functional requirements document is a critical component of the project scope, and any changes made to it can have a significant impact on the project's success. Therefore, it is important to have a formal change control process in place to manage any changes to the document. This process should include a mechanism for submitting change requests, evaluating the impact of the changes on the project, obtaining approval from relevant stakeholders, and updating the document accordingly. Putting the functional requirements document under change control helps to ensure that any changes made to the project scope are properly evaluated and approved. It also helps to prevent scope creep, which can lead to delays, budget overruns, and reduced project quality.

## Requirements Gathering for Systems Involving New Digital Technologies

The requirements gathering process can be especially challenging when it involves the implementation of new technologies. Users and stakeholders may not have a thorough understanding of the technical intricacies, the potential value that these innovations could bring, or how they could seamlessly integrate with the existing business processes. In such circumstances, the role of solutions architects becomes vital. They are required to bridge this knowledge gap and facilitate the successful translation of business needs into technical requirements.

Let's consider an example. Suppose a business is considering leveraging artificial intelligence to improve its customer service through chatbots. However, stakeholders may have a limited understanding of AI's potential, its functioning, or the effort required to integrate AI-based chatbots into their existing customer service processes. They may not be able to provide detailed requirements, such as the level of human-like interaction desired, the specific queries the chatbot should handle, or how the chatbot should interface with their existing customer relationship management system.

Similarly, the advent of blockchain technology has brought about vast potential for secure, transparent transactions and smart contracts. However, stakeholders may struggle to provide comprehensive requirements due to a lack of understanding of blockchain technology, its potential applications, and the technical challenges associated with its integration into current systems. For example, they may not realize the need to consider aspects like consensus algorithms, smart contract development, or the implications on data privacy regulations.

Solutions architects play a crucial role in this scenario. They should use their technical expertise and understanding of the business environment to guide stakeholders in articulating their requirements. Here are some strategies they can adopt:

- **Educate stakeholders:** Architects should take the initiative to educate stakeholders about the capabilities, limitations, and potential applications of the new technology in a language that they understand. This education can take the form of presentations, workshops, or hands-on demonstration sessions.

- **Showcase similar implementations:** Demonstrating case studies or examples of similar implementations can help stakeholders visualize the potential of the new technology and spur their thinking about their own requirements.

- **Use an iterative approach:** Given the uncertainties associated with new technology, it's wise to adopt an agile, iterative approach. Start with a basic implementation, gather feedback, and refine the requirements and the solution in subsequent iterations.

- **Facilitate brainstorming sessions:** Regular brainstorming sessions involving various stakeholders can help generate a wide range of requirements and ideas.

- **Prototype development:** Building a quick prototype of the proposed solution can help stakeholders better understand the capabilities of the technology and generate more specific requirements.

- **Leverage the expertise of technology vendors:** If the technology is being provided by an external vendor, leverage their expertise in understanding common use cases, potential pitfalls, and integration challenges.

Through these methods, solutions architects can bridge the knowledge gap, helping stakeholders articulate their requirements for implementing new digital technologies and ensuring a smoother transition during the integration process.

# Traditional Challenges with the Functional Requirements Process

Let's now review some common challenges that solutions architects have always faced and continue to deal with today. The process of gathering requirements, a crucial aspect of their role, has been practiced for many decades. Yet, many projects stumble or fail to meet business expectations due to hurdles tied to this critical process. Therefore, solutions architects must tread carefully when navigating this process. Here are some of the common challenges that solutions architects usually encounter during the requirement gathering phase.

- **Incomplete or vague requirements:** This is a significant issue that architects often face. Poor communication between stakeholders, a lack of understanding of business needs, or requirements that shift over time can all contribute to unclear or incomplete requirements. For instance, if a requirement only states "the system should be user-friendly," without specifying what that entails, it leaves too much room for interpretation, resulting in potential misunderstanding and failed implementation.

- **Scope creep:** Solutions architects may run into the issue of scope creep, which signifies the project requirements extending beyond the originally agreed-upon scope. This expansion could lead to delays, increased costs, and a compromised quality of the final product. For example, a software development project initially scoped for creating a simple website may gradually morph into a complex e-commerce platform, disrupting timelines and budget allocations.

- **Conflicting requirements:** Disagreements can arise when various stakeholders have different opinions about the project's objectives and scope. For example, the marketing team may desire a feature-rich website to attract customers, while the finance team might prefer a simpler, more cost-effective solution. This dichotomy can delay the project and create conflicts within the organization.

- **Changing requirements:** It's not uncommon for requirements to evolve during the development process, leading to extra costs, delays, and increased risks. For instance, a project initially aimed at creating an Android app might have to shift gears towards developing an iOS version due to changing market needs.

- **Stakeholder management:** Handling stakeholders can be a daunting task, especially when a project involves a large group of stakeholders with diverse interests, objectives, and expectations. An example of this challenge can be seen in an enterprise-wide software implementation, where everyone from the CEO to the frontline employees has a stake and different expectations from the solution.

- **Technical limitations:** Constraints such as hardware or software compatibility issues may also challenge the requirements gathering process. An ambitious AR project, for instance, may be hindered by the limitations of the currently available hardware or software frameworks.

- **Missing out on key stakeholders:** Overlooking any critical stakeholder can halt a project and cause severe disruption. As such, it's essential for the architect to meticulously identify all relevant parties when collecting requirements.

- **Incorrect information received from stakeholders:** It's fairly common for architects to receive erroneous requirements from some stakeholders, resulting in significant project rework. For instance, a stakeholder might request a particular feature without fully understanding the technical implications, leading to a lot of back-and-forth and wastage of resources. To mitigate this, architects should ensure that all collected requirements are extensively shared and validated by all involved parties. This rigorous process can unearth any inconsistencies or conflicts in requirements and help to address them before the development phase begins.

# Gathering Non-Functional Requirements

In addition to functional requirements, solutions architects should also gather non-functional requirements during the requirements gathering phase. Non-functional requirements refer to the technical and performance requirements that a digital solution must meet. These non-functional requirements include scalability, performance of the integrated system, reliability, security, business continuity, and so on. Each of the non-functional parameters should be designed by analyzing the system holistically and at each of the sub-components of the system.

The following are some of the typical non-functional requirements that are addressed when architecting cloud and digital solutions:

- **Security:** Digital solutions should have strong security measures in place to protect against data breaches, cyber attacks, and unauthorized access. Examples of security non-functional requirements include implementing multi-factor authentication, encryption of data at rest and in transit, and regular security testing.

- **Scalability:** Digital solutions must be scalable to accommodate growth and changing demand. Examples of scalability non-functional requirements include designing for horizontal scaling, implementing load balancers, and using cloud-based resources such as auto-scaling groups.

- **High availability:** Digital solutions must be highly available to users 24/7. Examples of availability non-functional requirements include designing for high availability, implementing disaster recovery solutions, and minimizing downtime during maintenance widows.

- **Performance:** Digital solutions must perform optimally and meet user expectations. Examples of non-functional requirements related to performance include setting response time targets, optimizing database queries, and implementing caching strategies. As another example, the design of an AI chatbot should ensure acceptable response times when responding to user inquiries. The chatbot should also be scalable to ensure that it can scale to handle many user inquiries without impacting the performance of the system. The chatbot should also be able to handle errors with ease and also handle irrelevant questions.

- **Reliability:** Digital solutions must be reliable and free from errors or bugs. Examples of reliability non-functional requirements include implementing fault tolerance, using automated testing, and establishing processes for monitoring and logging.

- **Usability:** Digital solutions must be easy to use and navigate for end users. Examples of usability non-functional requirements include following user interface design best practices, conducting user testing, and implementing accessibility standards.

By addressing these non-functional requirements when architecting digital solutions, solutions architects can ensure that the solutions are robust, scalable, and meet the needs of end users while adhering to industry best practices and standards.

## Gathering of Non-Functional Requirements

Non-functional requirements pertain to the expected behavior of a system rather than specific features. This includes attributes like security, usability, performance, reliability, scalability, and others. These requirements can be sourced from end users and can also be inferred from the technical infrastructure of the proposed solution.

End users can provide input on non-functional requirements based on their experience, needs, and expectations. For example, they might specify a need for a secure data handling system if they frequently deal with sensitive information. They might also express a preference for a user-friendly interface for easy navigation, or fast response times to ensure efficient task completion. These user-specified requirements are critical as they directly influence user satisfaction with the system.

In addition to user-specified requirements, solutions architects should also consider the technical aspects of the proposed solution to identify additional non-functional requirements. For example, if the digital solution will be hosted on a cloud-based infrastructure, architects might need to consider requirements around scalability and elasticity to handle varying workloads. If the solution involves integration with existing systems, there might be constraints around compatibility and interoperability that need to be considered.

Essentially, non-functional requirements derived from the technical solution ensure the system's optimal performance within the given architectural and infrastructural constraints, providing a robust, sustainable, and efficient digital solution.

Let's review an example to illustrate the various non-functional requirements related to a digital solution.

# Example: Non-Functional Requirements of an AR Application

For the AR application that was previously discussed, some examples of non-functional requirements could include the following:

Performance

- The AR application should provide fast and responsive performance to ensure a smooth and seamless user experience. Specifically, the AR application should load content within 2 seconds of a user command on a standard internet connection of 10 Mbps.

- The AR application should be able to load and display furniture images quickly and without delays. Specifically, the AR application should maintain a latency of less than 100 milliseconds during user interactions.

## Compliance

- The AR application should comply with all relevant data privacy regulations and protect customer data. Specifically, the AR application should comply with GDPR (for European Union customers), CCPA (for California, US customers), or other relevant regional data protection regulations.

- The AR application should ensure any data collection is done with the explicit consent of the user.

## Scalability

- The AR application should be able to handle a potentially large number of concurrent users without compromising performance or user experience. Specifically, the AR application should be designed to support up to 1 million concurrent users without degradation of performance.

- The AR application should be able to handle increasing volumes of furniture images as the retailer's product catalog grows. Specifically, the AR application should support a 50% increase in the volume of furniture images without requiring architectural changes.

## Reliability

- The AR application should be reliable and stable, with a high uptime and minimal downtime or system crashes. Specifically, the AR application should maintain a minimum of 99.95% uptime over a rolling 12-month period.

- The AR application should be able to recover within 2 hours of detection from any system failures or errors.

Security

- The AR application should protect customer data, such as their location and personal information, from unauthorized access or hacking attempts. Specifically, the AR application should use end-to-end encryption for all data transmissions to prevent data interception and misuse.

- The AR application should undergo regular (at least bi-annual) security audits and penetration tests to identify and resolve any potential vulnerabilities.

To ensure that non-functional requirements are comprehensive and complete, solutions architects should be specific, measurable, and in line with the needs of both the end users and the business. It's not enough to say that the application must be "fast" or "reliable." These attributes must be defined in concrete terms, such as latency times, uptime percentages, or data load capacities. Quantifiable objectives provide a clear target for the development team and set explicit expectations for stakeholders. Moreover, it is essential to consider all relevant facets of non-functional requirements including performance, compliance, scalability, reliability, and security. These areas encompass crucial aspects of user experience and satisfaction, as well as legal and operational considerations. Regular reviews and updates to these requirements will ensure the application remains relevant and effective in its operational context, while also responding adequately to emerging technologies, market trends, and regulatory changes.

# Best Practices for Achieving Business and Technology Alignment

Although We've covered some key processes where solutions architects can better align business and technology, there are additional best practices that can further enhance this alignment. It's essential to note that while the industry has long emphasized the importance of business and technology alignment, many organizations still grapple with this issue, especially when delivering digital solutions. Digital solutions are inherently more complex to design and implement than traditional IT solutions [8], necessitating a higher level of collaboration and alignment between business and technology teams. Failure to address this alignment can lead to a host of issues such as misaligned expectations, poor project outcomes, delays, and cost overruns.

The role of a solutions architect is critical in representing the technology/IT side of the project and working with the LOBs to ensure that their needs and requirements are met. However, the success of their interactions depends on various factors that can vary from one organization to another, such as the organizational structures, the role of the business in driving technology decisions, their level of influence in the process, and more.

These factors make it challenging to establish standard processes for interactions between business and technology, and require a tailored approach that takes into account the unique needs and circumstances of each organization. Effective communication, collaboration, and a shared understanding of goals and objectives are key to navigating these interactions successfully and achieving alignment between business and technology.

The following are some best practices related to solutions architecture that organizations can adopt to address alignment challenges between business and technology.

# Acting As a Technical Mentor and Advisor to the Business

Solutions architects should not just limit themselves to the task of gathering requirements, but also act as a technical mentor and advisor to the business stakeholders. They should be creative in their thinking and recommend innovative solutions that can help expand the horizons of the business.

As subject matter experts, solutions architects can bring a wealth of technical knowledge and experience to the table and can help the business stakeholders make informed decisions about technology-related matters. They can also provide guidance on emerging technologies, industry trends, and best practices, and help the business stakeholders stay ahead of the curve. By taking a proactive and consultative approach, solutions architects can establish themselves as trusted advisors to the business and help foster a culture of innovation and collaboration between business and technology.

Let's say that a retail company is looking to implement a new e-commerce platform to improve online sales. The solutions architect working with the business stakeholders can not only gather the technical requirements for the platform, but can also act as a technical mentor and advisor. For example, the solutions architect can recommend innovative features such as personalized product recommendations, real-time inventory tracking, and seamless integration with social media platforms. They can also provide guidance on the best technologies and frameworks to use for the platform, and help the business stakeholders understand the trade-offs and benefits of different options.

By taking this approach, the solutions architect can help the business stakeholders think more creatively about how they can use technology to enhance their business and provide them with the technical expertise needed to make informed decisions about the e-commerce platform. This can ultimately lead to a more successful implementation of the platform and a better overall experience for customers.

# Establishing Higher-Level Strategic-Level Agreements

The success of the day-to-day and operational interactions between IT and LOBs is greatly influenced by the strategic-level agreements (SLAs) and alignment between the technology leaders, such as the CIO, CTO, and other relevant managers, and the various LOB heads. Ideally, the senior leadership should define the overall relationship between the business units and the parameters of interaction to establish clear expectations and boundaries [9].

Let's say that a pharmaceutical company is developing a new drug to treat a particular medical condition. The IT department plays a crucial role in supporting the drug development process, such as managing the data from clinical trials, maintaining the electronic lab notebooks, and ensuring the security and privacy of the sensitive information.

However, the success of the IT department's day-to-day and operational interactions with the various LOBs, such as research and development (R&D), clinical operations, and regulatory affairs, is greatly influenced by the SLAs and alignment between the technology leaders and the LOB heads.

For example, the CIO, CTO, and other relevant managers may work with the R&D head to define the overall relationship between the IT department and the R&D team, such as the frequency and format of data updates, the data quality requirements, and the communication channels. They may also collaborate with the regulatory affairs head to establish the parameters of interaction, such as the data security and privacy policies, the compliance with the regulatory guidelines, and the risk management procedures.

By establishing clear expectations and boundaries, the IT department can effectively support the drug development process while also ensuring the integrity and security of the data. The IT department can work with the LOBs to provide the necessary technology solutions and services that meet their needs while also aligning with the overall goals of the drug development project.

Once these SLAs are established, the task of a solutions architect and the LOB representatives becomes much easier because they have a defined framework to work within. However, the responsibility to make these interactions and collaborations successful falls on the shoulders of the senior solutions architects and other relevant managers on both sides of the aisle. They must facilitate communication, collaboration, and alignment between the IT and LOB teams to ensure that they work towards common goals and objectives.

By fostering a collaborative environment and ensuring that both teams understand and work towards the same objectives, the IT and LOB teams can work more efficiently and effectively towards achieving business outcomes. This collaboration is crucial to the success of any organization, as it enables the IT team to provide technology solutions that are aligned with the business needs and goals.

# Engaging Closely with the Business Outcome Owners

While it's essential to involve all necessary business stakeholders to ensure that all requirements are captured and addressed, the solutions architect should particularly prioritize working closely with the business outcome owner. The business outcome owner is a stakeholder in a project who is responsible for defining the project's objectives and ensuring that they are achieved. They typically hold a senior leadership or management position in the organization and have the authority to make decisions regarding the project's scope, budget, and timelines. In most cases, they delegate this responsibility to the product owner, who works closely with the solutions architect and the technical team.

The solutions architect should clearly identify the business outcome owner and ensure that they are involved throughout the project's lifecycle. This includes regular communication and collaboration to ensure that the technical solution is meeting the business needs and that any changes to the solution are aligned with the project's goals.

By working closely with the business outcome owner, the solutions architect can ensure that the project is focused on delivering the desired outcomes and that the technical solution is designed and developed in a way that supports these outcomes. This collaboration is crucial to the success of the project, because it ensures that the solution meets the needs of the business and delivers the expected benefits.

# Improving Communication and Collaboration Between Technical and Business Teams

It's crucial for a solutions architect to understand the technical acumen of the LOB representatives they are working with. In some cases, the IT side may use technical jargon that's too complex for the business representatives, while on other occasions, the business side may struggle to explain their needs to the IT team. It's the responsibility of the solutions architect to facilitate clear communication between the two parties and ensure that everyone understands each other. This means finding a common language that everyone can understand and avoiding overly technical terms unless necessary.

# Working Closely with the Product Owner

Assessing the level of interaction required in gathering requirements is an important responsibility for solutions architects. In smaller projects where requirements are straightforward and do not significantly impact the technical architecture of the system, the product owner can collaborate with the development team to document requirements and create user stories without the involvement of a solutions architect.

However, in larger and more complex projects, involving a solutions architect is necessary to ensure that the requirements align with the overall technical architecture of the system and the enterprise architecture of the organization. The solutions architect is responsible for designing the technical solution and providing guidance on the overall system architecture, including integrating different components and technologies.

Therefore, the product owner should work with the solutions architect to define high-level requirements that align with the overall technical vision for the project. Once the solutions architecture is defined, the product owner can work with the development team to document granular requirements and create user stories based on the solutions architecture. This approach helps to ensure that the system is designed and developed to meet business needs while also being scalable, maintainable, and efficient.

# Project Deliverables (Business Alignment)

When collaborating with the business, a solutions architect is responsible for generating various deliverables to ensure the solution aligns with the organization's goals and addresses the identified needs. It's important to note that, ideally, the solutions architect will receive deliverables and documents such as the business architecture map and the business capability map as input from either the Enterprise Architecture department or the business/LOB itself, which will depict the current business state. These deliverables serve as valuable reference points for understanding the organization's existing capabilities, business processes, and strategic objectives. Insights derived from these deliverables enable the solutions architect to understand the business context, which subsequently enables them to design solutions that align with the organization's goals and effectively address the identified business requirements.

As for the particular deliverables produced by the solutions architect, they can vary based on the project's scope. Nevertheless, the following list showcases some common artifacts a solutions architect is likely to create while working alongside business stakeholders:

- **Business requirements analysis:** A comprehensive document capturing the business needs, functional and non-functional requirements, constraints, and assumptions for the proposed solution. This analysis helps in understanding the scope and objectives of the solution.

- **Stakeholder identification and analysis:** A list of key stakeholders involved in the project, including their roles, responsibilities, and expectations. This analysis helps in managing stakeholder communication and addressing their concerns throughout the project.

- **Business process modeling:** A representation of the current and future state of the business processes affected by the proposed solution. This may include process diagrams, flowcharts, or use case scenarios that help in understanding the impact of the solution on existing workflows.

- **Solution vision and scope:** A high-level description of the proposed solution's objectives, benefits, and key features. This document sets the direction for the solution and helps in communicating its value to stakeholders.

- **Risk assessment:** This documents the initial evaluation of potential risks and issues that may arise during the solution's implementation, along with strategies for mitigation and contingency planning. This assessment helps in proactively addressing potential challenges and ensuring a smoother project execution.

- **Preliminary cost-benefit analysis:** An estimation of the costs associated with implementing the proposed solution, as well as the expected benefits and return on investment (ROI). This analysis helps in making informed decisions about the feasibility and value of the solution.

# Summary

This chapter discussed the importance of business and technology alignment and the challenges that organizations face in achieving it. It highlighted the critical role of a solutions architect in bridging the gap between business and technology by working closely with both sides to ensure a successful outcome. The chapter emphasized that solutions architects need to act not only as technical advisors but also as strategic partners to the business. They should facilitate communication between highly technical teams and business users, and provide guidance on innovative solutions.

To achieve effective alignment between business and technology, organizations need to adopt best practices, such as involving business stakeholders early in the process, establishing clear ownership of business outcomes, and aligning technology goals with overall business objectives. The chapter emphasized that successful business and technology alignment requires continual collaboration and interaction between the solutions architect, business outcome owner, and technology leaders. By implementing these best practices and leveraging the expertise of solutions architects, organizations can successfully navigate the complex interactions between business and technology and achieve their desired outcomes.

# References

1.  Fujitsu Australia Limited. (2021). "Why do so many digital transformation projects fail?" Retrieved March 5, 2023, from `www.fujitsu.com/au/imagesgig5/211111_IA_WhyDoSoManyDigitalTransformationProjectsFail.pdf`

2.  Harvard Business Review. (2001). *Harvard Business Review on Aligning Technology with Strategy.* Harvard Business Review Press. Retrieved March 27, 2023, from `https://store.hbr.org/product/harvard-business-review-on-aligning-technology-with-strategy/10316`

3.  IMD Business School. (n.d.). "Business Strategy." IMD Reflections. Retrieved March 11, 2023, from `www.imd.org/reflections/business-strategy/`

4.  Business Architecture Community of Practice. (n.d.). "Definition of Business Architecture." Retrieved March 7, 2023, from `www.bacoe.org/definition`

5.  Business Architecture Associates. (2019). "Business Architecture Value Proposition." Retrieved from https://businessarchitectureassociates.com/wp-content/uploads/2020/10/5deecd9698d1d5cef8c9c313ea7b9316.pdf

6.  University of Houston-Clear Lake. (n.d.). "Business Use-Case Modeling." Retrieved from https://sceweb.uhcl.edu/helm/RationalUnifiedProcess/process/modguide/md_bucm.htm

7.  Do You Even ERP. (October 22, 2019). "Business Process vs Use Case." Retrieved from https://doyouevenerp.com/business-process-vs-use-case/

8.  Interfacing Technologies. (February 17, 2021). "Enterprise Architecture vs. Business Architecture." Retrieved from www.interfacing.com/enterprise-architecture-vs-business-architecture/

9.  Bughin, J., Catlin, T., Herring, P., & Kogan, J. (2018). "Managing Tech Transformations: Ideas, Insights, and Learnings from Leaders." McKinsey & Company. Retrieved March 27, 2023, from www.mckinsey.com/~/media/mckinsey/business%20functions/mckinsey%20digital/our%20insights/managing%20tech%20transformations/managing-tech-transformations.pdf

# CHAPTER 4

# Creating the Target Digital Technology Architecture

One of the main responsibilities of a solutions architect after gathering of business requirements is to create and maintain the target technical architecture for a given solution. This includes creating a comprehensive document that outlines the solution's applications, network, databases, and other infrastructure components. The target architecture document should also specify the overall integration strategy for the solution as a whole. This is a continuous process that requires ongoing attention and refinement throughout the project's lifecycle.

The target architecture document serves as a high-level architecture for the project, guiding the technical design and development of the technical team. In some projects, the high-level design and target architecture phases are combined into a single effort, which can result in the terms "high-level design" and "target architecture" being used interchangeably. Regardless of the approach, the target architecture document is a critical component of the project's success and should be continually reviewed and refined throughout the project lifecycle.

© Wasim Rajput 2023
W. Rajput, *Solutions Architecture*, https://doi.org/10.1007/978-1-4842-9657-8_4

# Example: Technical Architecture

As an example, the technical architecture for a digital online banking solution might include a multi-tiered structure with various interconnected components. The front-end layer could be built using a modern JavaScript framework like React or Vue.js for creating an intuitive and responsive user interface. This could communicate with a backend server layer, developed in a language such as Java or Python, which handles business logic and ensures data security. The back end could communicate with a database tier, managed by a system such as PostgreSQL or MySQL, for secure data storage and retrieval. Additionally, a microservices approach could be used, with individual services hosted on a cloud platform like AWS or Azure, all securely communicating through APIs. Identity and access management could be facilitated by OAuth or JWT-based security (OAuth stands for Open Authorization, which is a protocol that provides client applications a "secure delegated access" over HTTP to server resources on behalf of a resource owner; JWT, or JSON Web Token, is a compact, URL-safe means of representing claims to be transferred between two parties, often used for authentication and information exchange), ensuring secure user authentication and authorization. Lastly, continuous integration/continuous delivery (CI/CD) pipelines could be implemented for streamlined development, testing, and deployment.

While the aforementioned scenario provides a high-level overview of a potential technical solution, it's obvious that a multitude of underlying technical details need to be carefully defined and aligned. Crafting a robust and efficient technical architecture is not a straightforward endeavor; it requires navigating through a series of iterative and complex steps before it can be finalized. This process may involve in-depth requirements gathering, identifying and evaluating potential technologies and platforms, comprehensive system design, and thorough testing procedures. Furthermore, it requires diligent considerations around security, scalability, maintainability, and cost-effectiveness. Lastly, decisions must be influenced by the specific business needs, user expectations, and regulatory constraints of the industry in which the solution will operate. Thus, it's clear that while high-level architectural outlines provide a starting point, the intricacy and depth of the details required call for a structured, systematic, and expert-led approach and process to fully define the technical architecture.

The process of defining the target architecture typically involves several key steps. The typical steps are delineated below and illustrated in Figure 4-1.

Please note that this assumes that the solutions architect has a good grasp of the business requirements before embarking on these steps.

1. Conducting a current state analysis of the organization's technology architecture to understand the existing systems and infrastructure

2. Identifying the technology stacks that will be required for the new solution, considering factors such as functionality, scalability, security, and cost

3. Conducting feasibility studies and proof-of-concept (POC) tests for select areas of the project to test and validate the proposed solution's technical feasibility

4. Aligning the technical architecture with the organization's enterprise architecture (EA) to ensure consistency and adherence to the organization's overall technology strategy and standards

5. Creating the preliminary target architecture of the digital solution

6. Performing a risk analysis of the proposed architecture

7. Finalizing the target technology architecture of the digital solution

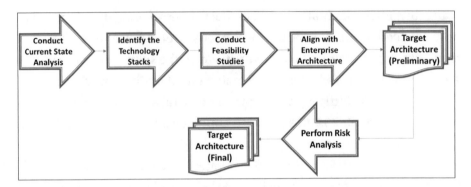

*Figure 4-1.* *Creating the solution's target technology architecture*

These steps not only help ensure that the target architecture is well-informed and well-aligned with the organization's needs and goals but that it also provides a solid foundation for the subsequent design and development phases of the project. By conducting a thorough analysis of the organization's existing architecture, identifying the necessary technology stacks required for the new solution, and validating the technical feasibility of the proposed solution, the team can move forward with confidence. This helps to minimize risks and reduce the likelihood of costly design changes or implementation delays down the road.

The upcoming sections of this chapter will provide a more detailed discussion of each of these steps.

# Conduct a Current State Infrastructure and Technology Assessment

One crucial step for a solutions architect before developing a target technology architecture for their solution is to conduct a current technology assessment of the overall environment related to the solution [1]. Performing a technology assessment of the current infrastructure can help the solutions architect gain insights into what's already in place, the related capabilities, and the additional capabilities that may be required to build the solution. This assessment enables the architect to identify any gaps or shortcomings in the existing infrastructure that may impact the success of the project. By gaining a better understanding of the current state of the technology environment, the solutions architect can develop a target architecture that aligns with the organization's overall technology strategy and goals while addressing any limitations or gaps in the current infrastructure.

# The Value of Performing Current Technology Assessment

Let's now cover specific scenarios where a current technology state assessment can be helpful toward the design and implementation of the new solution.

## Assessing Integration of the New Solution with the Current Environment

When building a new solution, one of the major challenges is integrating the new solution with the existing technology environment. This integration can involve complex technical and operational considerations that must be carefully managed to ensure a successful outcome. By performing a current technology assessment, a solutions architect can gain a deeper understanding of the integration challenges that may lie ahead and the steps that may be required to complete the integration. This assessment can help the architects identify any potential roadblocks and develop a comprehensive integration strategy that minimizes risks and maximizes the effectiveness of the overall solution.

Consider the introduction of an artificial intelligence solution within a healthcare organization, designed to aid in the diagnosis and treatment planning for patients. This AI system must integrate with existing electronic health record (EHR) systems, laboratory information systems (LIS), and imaging archives (like PACS). The challenge in this case lies not just in the technical aspects of dealing with different data formats and protocols, but also in the operational considerations such as ensuring data privacy and security in line with healthcare regulations like HIPAA. A current technology assessment could reveal challenges such as incompatible data structures between the AI and the EHR, or the need for robust anonymization procedures to protect patient data. These insights would allow the solutions architect to design an integration strategy that overcomes these obstacles, enabling the AI system to effectively aid clinicians without compromising patient privacy or the integrity of other systems.

## Identifying Similar Implementations in the Organization

In larger enterprises, it is not uncommon for a business and solutions architect to be unaware of similar solutions or technology implementations in other parts of the organization. To address this, the solutions architect can perform a discovery exercise to identify whether other teams are using similar technologies. By engaging with these teams and learning from their experiences, the solutions architect can benefit from the knowledge gained during their own development and implementation of solutions. This can help reduce duplication of effort, promote standardization, and ensure that the solutions architecture aligns with the organization's overall technology strategy. Moreover, by leveraging the expertise of other teams, the solutions architect can identify best practices and potential pitfalls that may impact the success of the project.

# Assessing the Security and Regulatory Compliance Status of the Current Environment

To ensure that the digital solution's target architecture adequately addresses the security and regulatory requirements of the new solution, the solutions architect must first gauge the security and regulatory compliance status of the existing overall environment. This assessment can help identify any gaps or weaknesses in the existing infrastructure that could impact the security or compliance posture of the new solution. By understanding the security and compliance status of the current environment, the solutions architect can develop the necessary controls and measures in their solution to address any shortcomings or gaps [2]. This ensures that the overall solution meets the necessary security and compliance standards and minimizes risks to the organization.

Let's take the case of a solutions architect developing a mobile banking application of a financial institution. During the assessment of the organization's existing technical infrastructure, the solutions architect may discover several vulnerabilities, such as outdated software and hardware, weak authentication mechanisms, and inadequate data encryption protocols. These vulnerabilities could expose the mobile banking application to security threats and regulatory violations. Based on this assessment, the solutions architect could implement the necessary controls and measures in the mobile banking application, such as two-factor authentication, robust encryption protocols, and secure data storage mechanisms, to ensure the security and privacy of customer data. This would ensure that the digital solution meets the necessary security and compliance standards and minimizes risks to the financial institution and its customers.

## Engaging with the Relevant Stakeholders

During the current technology assessment process, the solutions architect can also connect with other stakeholders in the organization and accordingly inform them of the plans for the new system or solution. This sharing of knowledge about the future can help surface any concerns earlier in the process, and prevent surprises later in the project. By engaging with stakeholders early, the solutions architect can identify potential roadblocks, obtain preliminary buy-in from stakeholders, and ensure that the overall solution is in line with the overall thinking of the organization's key stakeholders. This approach fosters collaboration and communication among different teams and departments, promoting a more cohesive and integrated approach to technology development and deployment.

## Planning Integration with the Operational Environment

Performing a current technical state assessment can help the solutions architect gain a better understanding of how their solution will fit into the organization's production environment. By analyzing the current operational technology landscape and infrastructure, the architect could identify any potential challenges or limitations that may affect the implementation and operation of the new solution. This assessment could then help the architect develop a plan that considers the existing infrastructure, applications, and processes, ensuring that the new solution integrates seamlessly with the production environment. By gaining a better view of the production environment, the solutions architect can design a solution that meets the specific needs of the organization and anticipate potential issues, resulting in a more efficient and effective solution.

For instance, envision a company that wishes to transition to a cloud-based data warehousing solution to enhance their data analysis capabilities. A solutions architect performing a current technical state assessment might discover that the existing on-premise servers run on outdated hardware and the data is stored in multiple disparate systems using different formats. Additionally, the company may lack established processes for data migration or have limited experience with cloud technologies. These findings indicate potential challenges such as the complexity of data consolidation, the need for data cleansing, the necessity for extensive staff training on cloud technologies, and the requirement for new data migration strategies. Based on this understanding, the architect could design a solution that not only includes the cloud-based data warehousing system, but also a comprehensive data migration plan, necessary staff training, and an ongoing data governance strategy. The architect's insight into the production environment, facilitated by the current state assessment, enables the creation of a solution that integrates smoothly with the existing infrastructure, accounts for its limitations, and meets the specific needs of the organization.

## Gaining Familiarity with the Organization's Technical Standards

A current technology assessment can also help the solutions architect become aware of any technology standards that may be in use within the organization. This knowledge can help them make informed decisions about the technologies and tools they select for their own digital solution. By aligning with the organization's technology standards, the solutions architect can ensure that their solution is compatible with existing systems and can minimize any potential conflicts or issues during implementation. Additionally, following technology standards can promote consistency, interoperability, and ease of maintenance across different systems and applications, which can improve overall system performance and reduce the cost of ownership over time. I will cover this point more later in this chapter under the topic of enterprise architecture (EA).

The above points illustrate some of the ways that performing technology assessments can be beneficial. By engaging with stakeholders early in the process, the solutions architect can prevent surprises and promote collaboration and design a solution that is better aligned with the current production environment. Organizational leaders should also encourage this practice to solicit more feedback on the current technology infrastructure, which can help them continuously optimize it.

# Defining the Scope of the Technology Assessment

One crucial step at the outset of a technology assessment is for the solutions architect to define its scope, essentially delineating the extent of its coverage. This is because it can significantly impact the depth and relevance of the assessment, ensuring it is focused on the most relevant aspects of the organization's technological landscape. It is imperative to limit the scope in such a way that while sufficient depth of analysis is achieved, the investment of time and resources is proportionate to the assessment's relevance and utility.

The current technology assessment is typically conducted as part of an enterprise architecture exercise, where a complete technology assessment is performed for the entire organization before creating a target technology state. If the organization has a well-established EA function, the solutions architect can leverage these findings, saving time for all involved. However, enterprise-wide assessments can take a long time, and the EA department may not conduct them frequently enough, leading to outdated documents as new systems are continually being implemented.

Therefore, the solutions architect needs to assess whether they can rely on previous assessment findings or whether they should perform their own current technology assessment. Additionally, they should define the assessment scope to ensure that it provides useful information on the organization's technology landscape and infrastructure while also being efficient with time. This approach ensures that the assessment strikes a balance between capturing the most relevant information and not spending more time than necessary.

The scope of a technology assessment thus can vary, ranging from a quick evaluation to a more detailed and thorough analysis. The solutions architect needs to decide the scope of the assessment based on the project's scope, complexity, business requirements, and affected stakeholders. For example, if the new system has higher stakes, they need to allocate more time to assess the current landscape thoroughly.

# Example: Technology Assessment for an IoT-Based System

Let's take the example of an IoT solution to understand what areas could be covered as part of a current technology assessment. IoT solutions typically involve a lot of devices and infrastructure components being used in many locations. For example, an IoT solution implemented within a manufacturing facility connecting to the central cloud could include a network of sensors and devices installed throughout the facility, such as temperature and humidity sensors, machine sensors, and RFID readers. These devices would communicate with a local gateway, which in turn would connect to the cloud for data processing and analysis. The cloud infrastructure would also include various services, such as data storage, analytics, and machine learning, which help extract meaningful insights from the data collected by the devices. Additionally, there may be a need for custom software applications or integrations with existing business systems to enable process automation and other features.

Although there are various dimensions that could be included in such a technology assessment, it could encompass some or all of the following areas:

- **Network assessment:** This involves analyzing the network architecture, such as network topology, bandwidth, and latency, to ensure that it can handle the data generated by the IoT devices. For example, the assessment should include the impact on local and enterprise networks due to the increased amount of traffic that will be generated over local networks as well as on the enterprise backbone. This can potentially strain the existing network resources. Making this part of the assessment can also help the organization's network architects plan for the deployment of the new solution.

- **Data storage requirements:** IoT devices and sensors can generate a substantial amount of data, which makes it essential to assess the organization's current storage architecture and resources. The assessment should ensure that the data generated by the IoT devices can be stored throughout the distributed architecture, including storage on the local edge cloud, central cloud, and other network locations where data may need to be accessed for analysis and decision-making.

- **Data management:** As IoT solutions rely heavily on data collection, storage, and analysis, it is crucial to perform a comprehensive data management assessment to understand how data is collected, stored, analyzed, and used within the organization. Specifically, the solutions architect's assessment should focus on how the new IoT system will generate data from IoT devices and how this data will need to be stored and processed across the overall information infrastructure of the organization.

- **IT infrastructure:** An understanding of the current IT infrastructure is essential to determine how the IoT solution will integrate with the existing technology environment. This includes evaluating the current hardware, such as servers, switches, and routers, to ensure that they are capable of supporting the new IoT devices. The assessment should also evaluate the current software, such as the operating systems, database management systems, and any manufacturing execution systems (MES), to ensure compatibility with the new IoT solution.

- **IT security:** Assessing the current IT security environment is crucial to identify potential risks and vulnerabilities associated with rolling out an IoT-based system. For example, communication channels between IoT devices and servers may be susceptible to interception and eavesdropping, leading to data breaches. Moreover, IoT devices can be hijacked and used to launch DDoS (distributed denial-of-service) attacks, overwhelming servers and causing downtime. Depending on the IoT solution and how it integrates with the organization's technology architecture, there may be several security concerns. Therefore, conducting a detailed security assessment can help illuminate the organization's current security policies, procedures, and technology infrastructure. The assessment can also identify any security gaps that need to be addressed before rolling out the IoT application to ensure that the system is secure and compliant with regulatory standards.

133

- **IoT communications protocols:** The solutions architect will need to ensure that the communications protocols used by IoT devices will be able to integrate with the current technology environment. These protocols define the rules and standards for how IoT devices communicate with each other and with other systems, such as cloud platforms and enterprise applications.

- **Power considerations:** The solutions architect will need to assess the power requirements of IoT devices at various locations and need to ensure that the current infrastructure can provide that extra power needed to operate that infrastructure.

The above are only some of the aspects that should be covered when performing a comprehensive technology assessment before the design and implementation of an IoT-based solution in a manufacturing facility. Other areas to consider include disaster recovery and availability, scalability, and performance of the existing infrastructure. Again, the specific scope of the assessment will depend on various factors such as the business requirements related to the new digital solution, the scope of the application, technologies used, and the organization's technology environment. The solutions architect should use their professional judgment to determine the appropriate scope for their assessment.

# Selection of Technology Stacks

A technology stack refers to the various technologies needed to architect, design, develop, deploy, and maintain the system. Before finalizing the target technology architecture, it is essential to identify and select the technology stacks that will be used in the design and implementation of the digital solution. This can include programming languages, software frameworks like microservices and containers, network technologies, databases, front-end and backend tools, and application integration technologies. The solutions architect is responsible for working with the full technical team to identify all the technology stacks required to build the solution [3].

Previous system implementations typically had simpler technology stacks, such as the LAMP stack comprising of Linux, Apache, MySQL, and PHP. However, with the proliferation of cloud-based technologies and services, the technology stacks related to delivering solutions are becoming increasingly complex. As a result, the solutions architect plays a critical role in ensuring the selection of the right mix of technologies (technology stack) that meet both the tactical and strategic needs of the organization. One example of a more recent technology stack is referred to as the MEAN stack. This technology stack consists of MongoDB NoSQL database, Express.js web framework, AngularJS front-end framework, and Node.js backend runtime environment. It is used for building dynamic web applications.

Given the criticality of the technology stack used in delivering digital solutions, the solutions architect must collaborate with other entities within the organization to ensure that the decision is reviewed by all relevant stakeholders. When selecting a technology stack, the solutions architect must address both the tactical and strategic needs of the solution. The tactical needs involve ensuring that the technologies can meet the requirements of the business problem that the solutions architect is attempting to solve. In this context, the selected technology stack should satisfy both the functional and non-functional requirements of the system. The strategic needs, on the other hand, involve ensuring that the selected technology stack can also support the future business applications based on the longer-term business architecture and strategy of the organization.

For example, if the system requires real-time data processing or a high degree of interactivity, a technology stack that includes in-memory databases would be better than traditional disk-based databases. Similarly, if the system needs to handle a large volume of user requests, a technology stack that includes load balancing and caching tools may be more appropriate than one that doesn't.

# Examples of Technology Stacks

Today's solutions typically require a technology stack that comprises both front-end and back-end components. Examples of technology stacks include

- UI (e.g., JavaScript)/Browser technologies (Bing, Safari, Chrome, etc.)

- Programming languages (Python, Java, etc.)

- Application development frameworks (e.g., Ruby on Rails, .NET, Spring)

- Software development kits (SDKs)

- Application runtime environments (Node.js)

- Networks

- Web servers

- Operating systems (Linux, Windows)

- Databases (relational databases, graph databases, key-value stores, etc.)

- Application integration technologies (APIs, message queues)

- Compute types (VMs, bare metal, containers, etc.)

- Storage types (block storage, file storage)

- Business intelligence tools

- And more

Moreover, each type of digital solution will have its own stack. For example, an IoT application stack will require software for device hardware, device operating system, device software, communications, cloud core services, and business and analytics applications. Similarly, an AI/ML application stack will require software for building data pipelines, ML pipelines, workflow management, tools for data storage, data cleansing, ML algorithms, model training, monitoring, and more.

The AWS data technology stack, on the other hand, is made up of a range of AWS services and technologies that can be used to build data solutions. This stack may include technologies such as Amazon EC2, a web service that provides secure, resizable compute capacity in the cloud; AWS Identity and Access Management (IAM), a web service that helps you securely control access to AWS resources; AWS Lambda, a service that lets you run code without provisioning or managing servers; and Amazon S3, an object storage service that offers industry-leading scalability, data availability, security, and performance.

In addition, this stack may also include Amazon DynamoDB, a key-value and document database that delivers single-digit millisecond performance at any scale; Amazon Redshift, a fully managed, petabyte-scale data warehouse service in the cloud; AWS CloudFormation, a service that provides a common language for organizations to describe and provision all the infrastructure resources in their cloud environment; and Amazon CloudWatch, a monitoring and observability service built for DevOps engineers, developers, site reliability engineers (SREs), and IT managers.

Similarly, a business intelligence and analytics application stack may include technologies such as Tableau, a powerful data visualization tool; IBM Cognos, a business intelligence and performance management software suite; MicroStrategy, a worldwide provider of enterprise analytics and mobility software; and other relevant software tools for data visualization, reporting, and analytics. And so on.

As you observe the variety of technology stacks and the inherent complexity in assembling them, it becomes evident that the solutions architect must employ a methodical approach in identifying and selecting the appropriate technologies prior to implementing any digital solution.

## Considerations When Selecting a Specific Technology Stack

The following are some of the key considerations when selecting technology stacks for the organization:

- **Future proofing:** The solutions architect is responsible for ensuring that the chosen technology stack is aligned with future technology trends and supports the strategic needs of the organization. Selecting the right technology stack is crucial if an organization expects its applications to scale over time or intends to use the technology stack in other solutions and applications. To mitigate the risks associated with technology stack selection, organizations can partner with cloud providers such as AWS and Azure, which are at the forefront of advanced technologies. Collaborating with these providers can help organizations stay up to date with the latest advancements and ensure that their services are built on reliable and thoroughly tested technologies.

- **Decision to go with the technology stack of one or more cloud providers:** When considering digital solutions, organizations should evaluate whether to work with a single cloud provider or multiple cloud providers. While working with a single cloud provider can simplify integration of different parts of a digital solution and reduce challenges for the architect when working with technology stacks from one provider, it can also lead to vendor lock-in. Therefore, deciding whether to use a single provider or multiple providers is a decision that requires careful consideration from both a business and technology standpoint.

- **Considerations for speed and agility:** The technology stack should enable accelerated technical design and development. For example, the selected technology stack should facilitate rapid application development and support quick iterations to meet evolving business and technology requirements. Additionally, the technology stack should allow for seamless integration with existing systems and tools. Selecting a technology stack that lacks integration capabilities may result in a costly and time-consuming effort to connect the new digital solutions with current business systems. Therefore, the available technical skills and expertise within the organization can be one of the factors that influence the decision to select a particular technology stack.

- **Vendor support:** To ensure the success of a digital solution, the solutions architect must verify that the selected technology stack has adequate support from the various technology vendors. For example, the solutions architect should ensure that none of the components of the technology stack are outdated or unsupported by the vendors. Additionally, when considering open-source technology stacks, the solutions architect should exercise caution as the level of support can vary significantly. As a result, the solutions architect should carefully consider the level of support available for each component of the technology stack and evaluate whether any potential risks associated with a lack of support are acceptable.

- **Maintenance and support:** In addition to verifying vendor support, the organization should ensure that the selected technology stack has an active community of developers and other technical resources who can provide the necessary ongoing support. A lack of skilled staff can lead to system downtime or delays in deploying upgrades and patches to address defects and other issues. Therefore, selecting a technology stack with an active community of developers and readily available technical resources can help ensure that the organization can address any issues that arise promptly and effectively.

- **Cost:** When selecting a technology stack, the solutions architect must also ensure that any cost implications are taken into account. For example, choosing a technology stack for the entire organization may require purchasing multiple licenses for specific tools and technologies. Additionally, some technology stacks may require specific infrastructure or hosting solutions, which can increase the overall cost of development and maintenance. For instance, selecting a technology stack that requires a particular type of server or cloud provider may result in higher hosting costs. Therefore, the solutions architect must carefully evaluate the costs associated with each potential technology stack and determine whether they are justifiable based on the benefits and value they provide to the organization.

The points mentioned above are merely a subset of considerations when selecting the technology stack for a given digital solution. Depending on the specific technical environment of the organization and the standards set by the EA department, there may be additional factors to consider. The solutions architect, therefore, should diligently compile this criteria, ensuring the relevance to the organization, prior to identifying and selecting the most suitable technology stack.

# Conducting POCs and Technical Evaluation of Tools and Services

Conducting Proof of Concepts (POCs) or prototyping is a critical activity in the solutions architecture process [4]. It is a useful way for the solutions architect to validate technologies and other components of a solution before finalizing the target technology architecture. The solutions architect utilizes POCs in the technical evaluation of tools and services that will be used throughout the project. In this capacity, the architect participates in all POCs and project trials, as well as in the development of a solution prototype. The ultimate objective of a POC is to provide the solutions architect, technical team members, and business stakeholders with increased confidence in delivering robust, reliable, secure, and high-performing digital solutions.

When conducting a POC, there are several considerations that a solutions architect should keep in mind. These include the following:

- **Choose a specific POC scenario:** Due to time and budget constraints, it may not be possible to conduct POCs for all scenarios. Therefore, the solutions architect should collaborate with all relevant stakeholders to determine which specific scenarios will be prioritized. The specific scenarios for a POC may include evaluating specific cloud services, testing the performance and scalability features of a particular technology, identifying migration challenges, validating technology capabilities, understanding the potential impact of a technology on an organization's operations and processes, and validating the scope of automation, among others.

- **Define the scope of the POC:** The next step is to further refine the scope of the POC and obtain agreement on it from all concerned stakeholders. It's important to note that while POCs are valuable in delivering digital solutions and can reduce overall implementation risk, they do require an investment of time and resources. If not controlled, this investment can begin to chip away at the project budget and distract the team from the main project goals, especially if the same team members are expected to work on both the POC and the project. Therefore, it's essential to be specific about the POC's scope and to agree with all stakeholders on the expected value of the POC.

- **Expanding the scope:** During the POC, stakeholders may decide to expand the scope of the project with each successful iteration. In some cases, the POC's scope can expand to become the actual scope of the project. As the POC progresses, stakeholders may discover new requirements, features, or functionalities that were not previously considered. These discoveries may lead to the expansion of the POC's scope, as stakeholders may want to explore and validate these new possibilities. This iterative approach can be beneficial as it allows stakeholders to refine and improve the concept gradually.

- **Conduct the POC in a controlled environment:** It is important to conduct the POC in a controlled environment with carefully selected data or processes to ensure that the results are reliable and can be used to make informed decisions about the viability of the technology or concept. The controlled environment helps to isolate the variables that could affect the results and ensures that the technology or concept is tested under consistent conditions.

Let's consider an example to demonstrate the value of conducting POCs in a controlled environment. Imagine an organization that is considering implementing an AI-based customer service chatbot on its website. This initiative represents a substantial investment of time, money, and resources, making it crucial for the organization to assess the feasibility and effectiveness of the chatbot through a POC. To conduct the POC, the organization decides to deploy the chatbot on a single page of the website, rather than the whole site, to gauge the chatbot's performance without disrupting the existing customer service ecosystem.

For the POC, the organization carefully selects a diverse range of common customer queries and complaints for the chatbot to handle. It also simulates peak load conditions to understand how the chatbot performs under stress. This method enables the organization to isolate critical variables, such as the complexity of customer inquiries and load conditions, and measure the chatbot's effectiveness, reliability, and scalability accurately. By conducting the POC in this controlled environment, the organization ensures the results are reliable and provide the information necessary to make an informed decision about the full-scale deployment of the chatbot technology.

- **Define the success criteria:** The solutions architect should also clearly define the success criteria for the POC and the specific decisions that are tied to the POC. These should be shared with the stakeholders. For example, when conducting an AI/ML application POC, a solutions architect may define success criteria related to testing the accuracy of the models on a specific data set (measured by metrics such as F1 score that measure's an AI model's accuracy, precision, or recall), measuring the percentage of correct predictions, measuring the difference between predicted and actual values, measuring the latency and response time of running the models, ability to handle large volumes of data, and the cost effectiveness of the overall process. This criteria should be agreed upon by all stakeholders before the POC is conducted.

After the POC is completed and the success criteria are met, the solutions architect should use the results to make informed architectural decisions. These decisions can be related to various aspects of the solution, such as technology selection, network topology, data storage, and data processing. For example, if the POC was conducted to test the feasibility of using a particular cloud service for a new solution, and the POC results showed that the service was able to meet the business objectives and success criteria, the solutions architect could decide to use that cloud service in the final architecture. Similarly, if the POC results showed that certain data processing or storage techniques were not feasible or scalable for the final solution, the solutions architect could decide to look for alternative solutions that better align with the business objectives and success criteria.

In conclusion, conducting a POC is a crucial step toward finalizing the target technology architecture of a digital solution. It provides a practical verification of the proposed solution's feasibility, effectiveness, and scalability in a controlled environment. The insights and data garnered through the POC allow organizations to make informed decisions and mitigate potential risks, ensuring that the selected technology aligns with the strategic objectives and technical environment of the organization. Therefore, a meticulously designed and executed POC is an invaluable component of a successful digital solution implementation.

# Solutions Alignment with Enterprise Architecture

Another crucial activity that the solutions architect engages in while architecting a digital solution is to ensure that the target solutions architecture of the project aligns with the target enterprise technology architecture. To accomplish this, the solutions architect must have a solid understanding of the fundamental principles of enterprise architecture and recommended activities for solutions architects to ensure alignment. It is important for the solutions architect to understand the overall EA strategy, the organization's goals and objectives, and the standards and guidelines for technology selection and implementation [5]. This understanding helps the solutions architect design solutions that are in line with the organization's EA strategy and technology standards, resulting in a more efficient and effective solution. By aligning the solutions architecture with the enterprise technology architecture, the solutions architect can also ensure that the digital solution meets the specific needs of the organization and can integrate seamlessly into the existing technology infrastructure.

As explained in earlier chapters, an organization's enterprise architecture comprises four dimensions: business architecture, technology architecture, information architecture, and application architecture (see Figure 4-2). In essence, the solutions architecture framework mirrors the overarching structure of the enterprise architecture. This reflects the notion that each digital solution, within the broader enterprise ecosystem, possesses its own distinct architectural elements. These encompass business architecture, application architecture, information architecture, and technology architecture tailored specifically to the solution. Thus, every digital solution, while contributing to the larger enterprise architecture, maintains its own unique set of architectural standards and structures. This alignment between solutions and enterprise architecture not only ensures consistency and interoperability across different solutions but also enables each solution to fully meet its specific requirements while contributing to the enterprise's overarching strategic goals. Figure 4-3 illustrates this concept.

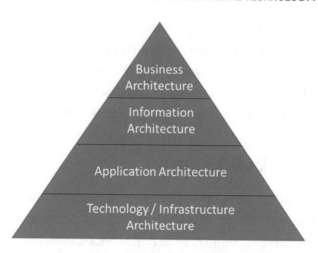

***Figure 4-2.*** *Dimensions of an organization's enterprise architecture*

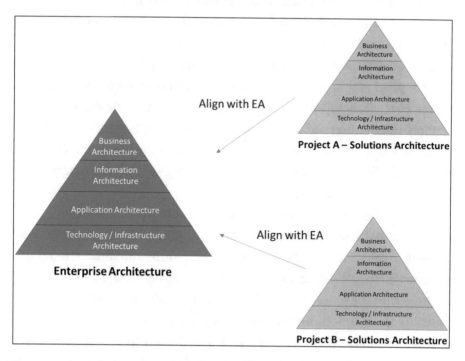

***Figure 4-3.*** *Alignment of various digital projects with an organization's EA*

In the previous chapter, I discussed steps that the solutions architect can take to align a digital solution with an organization's business architecture. In this section, I will focus more on aligning the solutions technology architecture with the other three dimensions of the enterprise architecture: technology, information, and application.

# Technology Architecture

Technology architecture refers to the structured organization or design of an enterprise's IT infrastructure, which includes hardware, software, networks, and other technology tools and services. It outlines how these components interrelate and function together to support the enterprise's goals and strategies. The focus is on providing a scalable, reliable, and efficient technology infrastructure that can effectively support the applications and data that the business relies on.

When evaluating a digital solution's technology architecture against the enterprise architecture, a solutions architect should consider several factors. First, the solutions architect should ensure that the digital solution's technology architecture aligns with the enterprise's overall technology strategy and goals. For example, the solutions architect should evaluate whether the digital solution's technology architecture supports the enterprise's cloud adoption strategy.

Second, the solutions architect should ensure that the solution's technology architecture aligns with the enterprise's overall infrastructure and network architecture. For example, the solutions architect should evaluate whether the digital solution's technology architecture can integrate with the enterprise's existing network infrastructure.

Third, the solutions architect should ensure that the technology architecture aligns with the enterprise's overall security and compliance requirements. For example, the solutions architect should evaluate whether the digital solution's technology architecture provides robust security features to protect enterprise data.

Last but not least, the solutions architect should ensure that the technology architecture aligns with the enterprise's overall performance and scalability requirements. For example, the solutions architect should evaluate whether the digital solution's technology architecture can scale to support the expected growth in users and data.

In many cases, solutions architects work with enterprise architects to ensure that new solutions align with enterprise architecture. However, enterprise architects can also learn from solutions architects, particularly when new technologies are introduced. In these situations, enterprise architects can work closely with solutions architects to evaluate new technologies and incorporate them into enterprise architecture. This allows other solutions architects in the organization to benefit from the same technologies if they are relevant to their respective solutions.

# Data Architecture

Data architecture pertains to the models, policies, rules, and standards that dictate how data is collected, stored, arranged, integrated, and used within an organization. It includes the design of data storage systems (like databases or data warehouses), data flows, and data governance. Its aim is to ensure data accuracy, consistency, security, and accessibility to support the organization's information needs and data-driven decision-making processes.

## Data Architecture vs. Information Architecture

Earlier, I stated information architecture as one of the building blocks of an organization's enterprise architecture. Although the terms "information architecture" and "data architecture" are sometimes used synonymously, in the realm of EA, they serve different yet complementary roles [6]. Data architecture pertains to the underlying structures, policies, storage, and movement of raw data within an organization, focusing on the design and organization of data storage systems, data flows, and data governance. On the other hand, information architecture concentrates on how processed data—information—is presented, organized, and made accessible to users, emphasizing usability, findability, and the understanding of data in a meaningful context. Both play integral roles in shaping how an organization manages and utilizes its data effectively.

While the enterprise architecture community differentiates between information architecture and data architecture, our focus in the context of building digital solutions will predominantly be with data architecture. This is mainly because data architecture involves the design and structuring of data, whether it's in transit or at rest, which is crucial for the creation of digital solutions. It governs how data is collected, stored, transformed, and integrated within the infrastructure, which directly influences the performance, scalability, security, and reliability of the digital solutions built on top of it. Given its foundational role in supporting the software layer, a robust data architecture is essential to ensure that the digital solutions are sustainable, adaptable, and efficient in meeting the evolving needs of the business.

When evaluating a digital solution's information architecture against the enterprise architecture, the solutions architect should consider several factors. First, the solutions architect should ensure that the information architecture aligns with the enterprise's data governance policies, standards, and practices. For example, if the enterprise has a specific data classification policy, the solutions architect should ensure that the digital solution's information architecture complies with this policy. A data classification policy is a set of guidelines and procedures that an organization implements to classify its data into different categories based on its level of sensitivity, importance, and regulatory requirements [7].

Second, the solutions architect should ensure that the digital solution's information architecture integrates seamlessly with other enterprise systems and applications. For example, the solutions architect should ensure that the digital solution's information architecture can share data with other enterprise applications without any issues.

Third, the solutions architect should ensure that the information architecture aligns with the enterprise's data architecture, metadata management practices, and scalability and performance requirements. For example, the solutions architect should evaluate whether the digital solution's information architecture can scale to handle large volumes of data.

Fourth, the solutions architect should ensure that the information architecture complies with the enterprise's data security policies and standards. For example, the solutions architect should evaluate whether the digital solution's information architecture encrypts sensitive data as required by the enterprise's security policies.

Finally, the solutions architect should ensure that the information architecture aligns with the enterprise's data management and governance practices. For example, the solutions architect should evaluate whether the digital solution's information architecture supports the enterprise's data retention and archiving policies. By considering these factors, the solutions architect can ensure that the information architecture of the digital solution aligns with the enterprise architecture and meets the needs of the enterprise.

# Application Architecture

Application architecture focuses on the high-level structure of software applications and how they interact with each other to support business processes. This includes the selection of software technologies, the design of software components, and the definition of interfaces and data flows between components. It ensures that the organization's applications are scalable, reliable, secure, and able to meet the needs of the organization.

When evaluating a digital solution's application architecture with the enterprise architecture, a solutions architect should consider several factors. To begin, the solutions architect should first ensure that the application architecture adheres to the enterprise's application architecture standards and guidelines. For example, if the enterprise's application architecture recommends the use of microservices architecture, the solutions architect should ensure that the digital solution's application architecture follows the same pattern.

Next, the solutions architect should evaluate the application's integration capabilities to ensure that it can seamlessly integrate with other enterprise applications. For example, if the enterprise uses a specific middleware solution, the solutions architect should ensure that the digital solution's application architecture can integrate with the middleware.

The solutions architect should also consider the application's scalability and performance characteristics to ensure that it can handle the enterprise's current and future needs. For example, the solutions architect should evaluate the application's ability to handle increasing volumes of users and data.

The security of the application is another critical area that requires evaluation. The solutions architect should evaluate the application's security features to ensure that it meets the enterprise's security policies and standards. For example, if the enterprise requires the use of multi-factor authentication, the solutions architect should ensure that the digital solution's application architecture supports this feature.

Finally, the solutions architect should consider the application's maintenance and support requirements to ensure that it aligns with the enterprise's IT support structure. For example, the solutions architect should evaluate whether the enterprise has the necessary resources to maintain and support the digital solution's application architecture.

## Summary

In summary, a comprehensive understanding of the enterprise architecture is essential for the creation of digital solutions that align with the business objectives and the technical strategy of an organization. By keeping a keen eye on how the technology, data, and application architectures align with the overarching EA, solutions architects can design digital solutions that not only fit into the existing IT landscape but also drive the business forward by leveraging the right technologies, managing data efficiently, and building applications that cater to the specific needs of the organization. This practice contributes to a more efficient, secure, and scalable digital ecosystem, helping organizations achieve their strategic goals while minimizing potential technical debt (covered in the next chapter). Through this meticulous alignment process, solutions architects also demonstrate the value of a well-executed EA, underlining its importance in steering the organization's digital journey.

# Developing the Solution's Target Technology Architecture

The previous section shed light on the importance of aligning a digital solution with an organization's EA. This section, however, delves into the creation of the actual technical architecture of the digital solution itself. Composed of three main constituents—data architecture, application architecture, and technology/infrastructure architecture—the technical architecture forms the foundation of any digital solution. It lays out the underlying technology infrastructure, designs the way data is managed and utilized, and delineates the high-level structure of software applications and their interactions. Crafting this technical architecture is an intricate but crucial task, as it directly impacts the solution's performance, scalability, security, and overall ability to meet the business requirements effectively.

Additionally, it is important to note that security architecture is an integral part of this technical architecture, enforcing protocols to safeguard data and system integrity, thereby ensuring the resilience and trustworthiness of the digital solution. I will, therefore, discuss that dimension as well in the context of creating a digital solution's target technology architecture.

The following sections will cover each of these domains in detail.

# Technology and Infrastructure Architecture

Developing the solution's target technology architecture involves creating a comprehensive blueprint that outlines the desired end state of the technology infrastructure supporting the digital solution. It outlines a detailed architecture of infrastructure resources that will be required for the digital solution. It addresses the various hardware and virtual components needed to operate the digital solution along with defining their connectivity, interfaces, configuration, and other aspects. The target technology architecture should also incorporate best practices in infrastructure automation, DevOps, and monitoring to ensure efficient deployment, management, and continuous improvement of the digital solution. When working on the technology infrastructure dimension of digital solutions, several key aspects must be considered to ensure the effectiveness and scalability of the system. Here are some key dimensions with short examples for each in the context of digital solutions:

- **Compute resources:** Determine the type and scale of compute resources needed to support the digital solution's processing requirements. For example, in a digital video streaming platform, suitable virtual machines or container-based solutions with adequate processing power must be selected to handle video transcoding and streaming tasks.

- **Storage resources:** Evaluate the storage capacity, performance, and types required to handle the digital solution's data needs. For example, in a digital document management system, a combination of fast SSD (solid-state drive) storage for frequently accessed files and cost-effective object storage for archiving older documents may be selected.

- **Networking:** Design the network architecture to ensure high availability, low latency, and secure communication between the digital solution's components. For example, in a digital gaming platform, a content delivery network (CDN) can be implemented to reduce latency for players, and a secure virtual private network (VPN) can be used for backend management.

- **Scalability and elasticity:** Design the infrastructure to scale horizontally or vertically based on the digital solution's changing demands. For example, in a digital e-commerce application, auto-scaling groups in a cloud environment can be used to handle traffic spikes during seasonal sales or promotional events.

- **High availability and fault tolerance:** To ensure high availability and fault tolerance, redundancy and resilience must be incorporated into the infrastructure to minimize downtime and maintain service continuity. For instance, in the case of a digital finance application, a multi-region or multi-zone deployment with load balancing and failover mechanisms must be implemented.

- **Monitoring and management:** Establish monitoring, logging, and alerting solutions to track the health and performance of the infrastructure and implement management tools for efficient administration. For example, in the case of a digital marketing automation platform, this could involve using cloud-based monitoring and logging services to track infrastructure metrics and a centralized configuration management system for updates and deployments.

- **Cloud and hybrid infrastructure:** Determine the optimal mix of cloud-based, on-premises, and hybrid infrastructure to meet the digital solution's needs in terms of cost, performance, and compliance. For example, in the case of a digital manufacturing system, one could use a hybrid infrastructure approach that combines on-premises edge computing for real-time processing with cloud-based resources for data storage and analytics.

- **Infrastructure automation and DevOps:** Implement automation and DevOps practices to streamline infrastructure provisioning, deployment, and management, improving efficiency and agility. For example, in a digital customer support platform, a solutions architect could use Infrastructure as Code (IaC) tools to automate the provisioning and configuration of virtual machines or containers, and CI/CD pipelines for rapid deployment of application updates.

- **Integration with third-party services:** Ensure seamless integration with external services and APIs that the digital solution may depend on for additional functionality or data. For example, in the case of a digital travel booking platform, this may involve integrating with third-party APIs for flight data, hotel information, and payment processing services.

In conclusion, the creation of a target technology/infrastructure architecture for a digital solution requires the identification and specification of infrastructure resources plus meticulous consideration of critical factors like compute resources, storage, networking, high availability, fault tolerance, monitoring, management, infrastructure automation, and more. The embodiment of these factors within the technical architecture directly impacts the performance, security, scalability, and overall capability of the digital solution. Therefore, it's imperative to ensure they are methodically addressed and effectively integrated, resulting in a digital solution that aligns with the organization's EA and fulfills the business requirements efficiently and effectively. The aforementioned dimensions and related examples shed light on how these aspects can be realized in the context of different digital solutions.

# Creating the Application Architecture

As mentioned, application architecture refers to the various technologies, architectural patterns, and styles used to design an application. Based on the functional and non-functional requirements, as well as enterprise architecture standards and guidelines, the solutions architect selects the most suitable application architecture for the digital solution. Below are some of the topics relevant to a cloud-native application architecture. The specific application architecture ultimately chosen for any given solution will depend on several factors that include the technology stacks chosen, the characteristics of the digital solution being developed, the business requirements, and even the project constraints such as timeline and budget. Therefore, it's essential to remember that the architectural principles should be tailored and adapted to fit the unique context and needs of each individual project.

- **Identifying the different application domains:**
  A large digital solution may have several domains, which an application architect must identify as part of developing the application architecture. By identifying the specific domains that the application will need to support, the application architect can determine

which applications are needed to support a larger solution and design an application architecture that meets the needs of the organization. For instance, if the application is designed to support a business domain such as accounting, it may require applications such as accounting software, financial reporting tools, or business intelligence systems. Similarly, if the application is designed to support a business domain such as sales, it may require applications such as customer relationship management (CRM) software, sales tracking tools, or e-commerce platforms. By identifying the specific domains and the applications needed to support them, the architect can ensure that the application architecture is properly designed and integrated to achieve the desired functionality, performance, and security of the application.

- **Architectural styles:** Applications can be designed with varying styles, such as client-server, object-oriented, or microservices-based architecture. A solutions architect works with the technical teams to decide on the architectural styles used in the solution design. These styles may apply to the overall application or to smaller sections of the application with different styles. For instance, a digital banking solution might employ a microservices-based architecture for the backend operations to facilitate independent scaling and deployment of different services, such as account management, funds transfer, or loan processing. On the front end, a client-server architecture might be implemented to separate concerns between the user interface and data retrieval mechanisms. This could involve the use of web technologies such as JavaScript and HTML for client-side operations and a language like Python or Java for server-side processes. Moreover, within a specific microservice, object-oriented design principles might be used to structure the code in a way that promotes encapsulation, inheritance, and polymorphism, enhancing modularity and code reusability. Therefore, the choice of architectural styles reflects a mix-and-match approach, optimizing each section of the application to meet specific functional requirements, non-functional requirements, and technological constraints.

- **Architectural layers:** For applications within the digital solution, designs are required for various layers, such as presentation services (e.g., UX), business services (including business entities, logic, rules, etc.), data, and internal services. For instance, in a digital banking application, the architectural layers include a user-friendly presentation layer, a business services layer that encapsulates banking operations, a data layer that handles storage and manipulation of data, and an internal services layer providing support functions such as authentication. When appropriately designed, these layers contribute to a robust, efficient, and secure digital solution that meets business needs while enhancing user experience.

- **Microservices architecture:** This involves designing applications as a collection of loosely coupled services, which can be developed, deployed, and scaled independently. For instance, consider an e-commerce application, which could be divided into several microservices such as user management, inventory management, order processing, and payment processing. Each of these services operates independently of the others, yet they communicate and collaborate to provide a complete e-commerce experience. This design enables teams to develop and update services independently, deploy them without disrupting the entire application, and scale specific services based on demand, resulting in increased agility and improved resilience.

- **Integration and application-level communications:** This covers the integration of various application components with each other and external systems. It encompasses the dependencies and integrations within different components, along with APIs, API gateways, service meshes, and message queuing architectures employed for application and service-level communications. For instance, adopting a RESTful API-driven approach facilitates communication between application components and external systems, ensuring loose coupling and promoting easier, independent component evolution.

- **Application architecture parameters:** At a lower level, an application architecture needs to account for various architectural issues, such as application authentication and authorization methods, caching technologies and mechanisms, exception management, logging, data access, and handling of concurrent transactions.

- **Choosing the right cloud service model:** This refers to selecting between Infrastructure as a Service (IaaS), Platform as a Service (PaaS), or Software as a Service (SaaS) based on the application's requirements and the level of control and management that the organization wants to retain.

- **Designing for statelessness:** This is about ensuring that application components can handle requests without relying on the previous state of the system. This allows for better scalability and fault tolerance. For instance, in a digital e-commerce platform, stateless application design can ensure that individual components, like product catalog or shopping cart, can handle user requests without depending on previous interactions. This promotes better scalability during high-traffic periods and robust fault tolerance, as failure in one component doesn't disrupt the entire system's functionality.

- **Leveraging managed services and serverless technologies:** An organization can utilize managed services like databases, messaging systems, and machine learning to offload operational tasks to the cloud provider. For example, one could consider serverless technologies like AWS Lambda or Azure Functions for event-driven, on-demand computation.

- **Optimizing for scalability and performance:** One can design the application to handle varying loads and scale horizontally by adding or removing instances as needed. This also includes consideration for the use of caching, content delivery networks, and other techniques to improve performance and reduce latency.

161

- **Designing for cost optimization:** Keeping cloud costs in check by selecting the right resources, using autoscaling, and following best practices for cost management is an important consideration when developing an application architecture.

These are some of the key areas that need to be taken into account while designing an application architecture for a given digital system. Again, although these areas are crucial, the actual domains to be addressed may vary depending on the scope of the digital solution.

# Creating A Data Architecture

Data architecture encompasses the models, policies, rules, and standards that govern how data is collected, stored, processed, and used within an organization or system. It plays a crucial role in the design of digital solutions by ensuring data integrity, consistency, security, and accessibility, ultimately enabling businesses to make data-driven decisions, optimize operations, and provide enhanced user experiences. A well-designed data architecture supports scalability, performance, and adaptability to evolving requirements, allowing digital solutions to accommodate growth and respond to changing business needs while maintaining data quality and compliance with relevant regulations.

Similar to other areas of the architecture, finalizing an application's data architecture requires careful planning and consideration of several factors. Here are the high-level dimensions that data architects should address, especially in the context of digital solutions:

- **Data sources and integration:** This involves identification and understanding of the various data sources, both internal and external, that the digital solution will rely on. The architect should design mechanisms to integrate these data sources, ensuring the seamless flow of data between systems and addressing issues like data format, consistency, and latency. For example, in a digital health platform, integrating data from electronic health records (EHRs), wearable devices, and third-party health services requires a robust data ingestion pipeline that can handle various data formats and maintain data consistency.

- **Data modeling and storage:** This refers to designing data models that accurately represent the application's data entities, attributes, and relationships. One should select the appropriate storage technology based on the application's requirements, such as relational databases, NoSQL databases, data warehouses, or object storage. The architect should also consider factors like data consistency, scalability, and querying capabilities. For example, for a digital banking application, designing relational data models and schemas to represent customers, accounts, and transactions, and storing them in a high-performance relational database such as PostgreSQL or MySQL is crucial for data integrity and efficient querying.

- **Data processing and analytics:** This refers to the design of processes and systems for data processing, transformation, and analysis. This may involve batch processing, real-time data processing, or a combination of both. One should also plan for integration with data analytics, machine learning, and reporting tools to support data-driven decision-making. For example, when working on a digital marketing solution, implementing real-time data processing and data analytics pipelines using technologies like Apache Kafka and Apache Flink enable capabilities such as the immediate analysis of customer behavior, enabling personalized marketing campaigns and recommendations.

- **Data security and privacy:** This refers to implementing data security measures to protect sensitive information and ensure compliance with data protection regulations and privacy laws. This may involve encryption, access controls, data masking, and proper data handling, storage, and retention policies. For example, for a digital identity management system, implementing strong data encryption at rest and in transit, role-based access controls, and anonymization techniques is essential to protect users' sensitive personal information and to comply with data protection regulations.

- **Data governance and quality:** This refers to establishing data governance policies and practices to maintain data quality, consistency, and accuracy. This also involves implementing data validation rules, deduplication methods, and cleansing processes to improve data quality. For example, in the case of a digital supply chain management platform, establishing data validation rules, deduplication processes, and a data catalog helps maintain data quality and accuracy, ensuring that stakeholders can trust the insights derived from the system.

- **Performance and scalability:** This involves optimizing the data architecture to handle varying workloads, ensuring low-latency data access, and scale as needed. It also involves employing techniques like caching, data partitioning, and sharding to distribute data and improve performance. For example, for a digital streaming service, optimizing the data architecture using caching, data partitioning, and sharding ensures low-latency access to content metadata and user information, providing a seamless user experience even during peak usage periods.

- **Data backup and disaster recovery:** This is about developing a comprehensive data backup and disaster recovery strategy to minimize data loss and ensure business continuity. This includes creating redundant data copies, utilizing backup storage solutions, and defining recovery point objectives (RPO) and recovery time objectives (RTO) based on the application's criticality and tolerance for data loss. For example, in a digital e-commerce platform, implementing a comprehensive backup strategy with regular data snapshots, geo-redundant storage, and well-defined RPOs and RTOs ensures minimal data loss and rapid recovery in case of system failures or data center outages.

- **Data interoperability and standardization:** This ensures data compatibility and interoperability among different systems and applications by adopting standardized data formats, protocols, and APIs. This promotes seamless data exchange and integration across various components of the digital solution. For example, when designing a digital smart city solution, adopting standardized data formats, protocols, and APIs, such as JSON or XML, and using open data exchange standards like Open311 or GTFS (General Transit Feed Specification), ensures seamless data exchange and integration across various city systems and applications.

These are some of the key areas that need to be taken into account while designing a data architecture for a digital system. Although these areas are crucial, the actual domains to be addressed may vary depending on the scope of the digital solution.

## Example: Data Architecture Consideration When Working on AI/ML Systems

Let's take an example of a data architecture for a digital solution involving AI/ML. In such cases, data architects should take into account the following aspects:

- **Data preparation and preprocessing:** Machine learning models require high-quality, well-structured data for training and validation. Data architects should design processes for data cleaning, normalization, and feature extraction to ensure that the data is suitable for ML algorithms.

- **Model training and deployment:** Data architects should consider the infrastructure requirements for training and deploying ML models, such as specialized hardware (e.g., GPUs or TPUs) and scalable cloud-based resources. They should also establish a pipeline for continuous integration and deployment of ML models, enabling rapid iteration and improvement.

- **Model monitoring and management:** Once deployed, ML models need to be monitored for performance, drift, and potential bias. Data architects should design mechanisms for tracking model performance, updating models when necessary, and maintaining transparency and explainability in the AI systems.

- **Real-time data processing and analytics:** Solutions that require real-time data processing and analytics demand a data architecture that can handle high-velocity data streams and deliver insights with low latency.

- **Data streaming and ingestion:** This refers to selecting appropriate data streaming technologies, such as Apache Kafka or AWS Kinesis, to handle the ingestion of high-velocity data streams and designing a scalable and fault-tolerant data ingestion pipeline that can process and store incoming data efficiently.

- **Integration with downstream systems:** Real-time insights generated by the stream processing system may need to be integrated with downstream applications, databases, or visualization tools. Data architects should ensure seamless integration and communication between these components while maintaining data consistency and integrity.

By addressing such dimensions, data architects can design effective and scalable data architectures for digital solutions involving new digital technologies, ensuring that the systems can handle evolving requirements and deliver the desired outcomes.

# Creating the Security Architecture

Digital solutions are becoming increasingly ubiquitous in modern business operations, and with this comes the need for robust security architecture. The objective of security architecture is to identify and address any security vulnerabilities in a digital solution, ensuring that sensitive data is safeguarded and protected against cybersecurity threats. Organizations must be aware of the latest cybersecurity threats when implementing digital and cloud solutions and develop security architecture to mitigate those risks [8].

## Common Security Threats

Here are some of the common threats to consider and the actions that can be taken from a security architecture perspective to protect against them.

- **Phishing attacks:** Phishing attacks are a form of social engineering in which cybercriminals use emails or other means to trick individuals into providing sensitive information such as login credentials or credit card numbers. To mitigate this risk, security architecture should include strong authentication mechanisms such as two-factor authentication and employee training to help them recognize and avoid phishing emails.

- **Ransomware:** Ransomware is a type of malware that encrypts data on a computer or network, making it inaccessible until a ransom is paid. To mitigate this risk, security architecture should include regular data backups, network segmentation to limit the spread of ransomware, and security tools such as antivirus software and intrusion detection systems.

- **Insider threats:** This pertains to the potential danger presented by individuals such as employees, contractors, or other authorized personnel who have access to an organization's data and systems. In order to reduce this risk, it is important for the security architecture to incorporate access controls and monitoring tools that can detect and prevent unauthorized access or the transfer of data outside of the organization.

- **Supply chain attacks:** Supply chain attacks occur when a cybercriminal targets a third-party vendor to gain access to an organization's systems and data. To mitigate this risk, security architecture should include regular assessments of third-party vendors and their security controls.

- **Cloud misconfiguration:** Cloud misconfiguration refers to the incorrect or incomplete implementation of security controls in cloud-based systems, which can leave them vulnerable to attack. To mitigate this risk, security architecture should include regular security assessments and auditing of cloud-based systems to ensure that security controls are properly implemented and configured.

In summary, to mitigate cybersecurity threats when implementing digital and cloud solutions, security architecture should include a combination of technical controls, employee training, and regular security assessments and monitoring. It is also essential to stay up to date with the latest cybersecurity threats and to adapt security architecture accordingly to address new and emerging risks.

# Security Controls

To mitigate the potential security vulnerabilities in a digital solution, several controls should be considered when developing security architecture. The controls typically fall into the following areas:

- **Authentication and authorization:** Authentication is the process of verifying the identity of a user or a device, while authorization is the process of granting or denying access to resources based on the authenticated identity. In digital solutions, authentication and authorization are critical components of security architecture, and solutions architects must ensure that appropriate measures are in place to safeguard sensitive data and ensure that only authorized personnel can access it. For example, in an e-commerce system, users must be authenticated before accessing their account and making purchases.

- **Encryption and data protection:** Encryption is the process of converting plaintext into ciphertext, which is unreadable without the correct decryption key. Data protection involves securing data from unauthorized access, use, disclosure, or destruction. In digital solutions, encryption and data protection are necessary to prevent data breaches and protect sensitive information. For example, in an AI/ML system, sensitive data must be encrypted to prevent unauthorized access or manipulation.

- **Network security:** Network security involves protecting the network infrastructure and its assets from unauthorized access, use, disclosure, or destruction. In digital solutions, network security is critical to protect against cyber-attacks such as DoS attacks and data breaches. For example, in an IoT system, network security is necessary to protect against unauthorized access and control of IoT devices.

- **Security monitoring and incident management:**
  Security monitoring involves the continuous monitoring of systems, networks, and applications to identify potential security threats or incidents. Incident management involves responding to security incidents and taking appropriate actions to mitigate the impact of the incident. In digital solutions, security monitoring and incident management are necessary to detect and respond to security incidents in a timely and effective manner. For example, in a blockchain system, security monitoring and incident management are critical to detect and respond to potential attacks on the blockchain network.

- **Compliance and risk management:** Compliance involves ensuring that a digital solution complies with applicable laws, regulations, and standards. Risk management involves identifying, assessing, and mitigating risks associated with the digital solution. In digital solutions, compliance and risk management are necessary to ensure that the solution is secure and that the organization is not exposed to legal or financial risks. For example, in an IIoT system, compliance and risk management are necessary to ensure that the system complies with industry standards and regulations and that the organization is not exposed to financial or legal risks.

Given the above scenarios, it is obvious that in today's digital age, security architecture is more important than ever before. A comprehensive security architecture approach, therefore, can help organizations stay ahead of the ever-evolving cybersecurity landscape, providing them with the necessary safeguards to protect their digital solutions and overall enterprise.

# Target Technology Architecture Risk Assessment

Once the preliminary target architecture for a digital solution is prepared, the solutions architect should conduct a detailed risk assessment related to the architecture before finalizing it. While digital and cloud-based solutions offer numerous growth opportunities, they also pose challenges and risks that need to be addressed to ensure the overall stability of operations and the business. Addressing these risks may require additional investment and time, which the solutions architect must factor into the overall delivery plan. Without proper risk management, the overall architecture of the solution and its delivery plan may not be complete, which can have a direct or indirect impact on the project's success [9].

## Examples: Technology Risk Assessment

The importance of a technology risk assessment can be highlighted using an example. Let's consider an organization that plans to use a multi-region architecture to facilitate its global expansion and high availability. While the AWS cloud provides a multi-region infrastructure that allows businesses to deploy applications across multiple geographic regions, a solutions architect may discover that the basic architecture may not be suitable for the organization's use cases and can lead to several implementation risks. For instance, some of the challenges associated with multi-region architectures include data replication, uniform configuration management, latency issues, and cross-region networking. Addressing these issues may require the use of additional AWS services, such as AWS Global Accelerator and AWS Transit Gateway, and implementation of other best practices recommended by Amazon for securing multi-region architectures. However, such an approach may add to the overall cost of the project and increase testing and deployment time. Therefore, the solutions architect should conduct a detailed risk assessment related to the architecture before finalizing it, and factor in the additional investment and time required to mitigate the associated risks.

Similarly, a solutions architect working on the design and implementation of a computer vision project may identify the following risks, which could impact the successful completion of the overall project:

- An organization may not have the data quality that may be needed to train a computer vision project. A system trained on bad quality data will obviously produce bad results and impact its overall accuracy.

- The system may be difficult to scale or may be costly for the organization due to the large volume of data that could be produced.

- The maintenance of the project may be difficult due to lack of skills and staff that could threaten the longer term sustainability of the project.

- The complexity of the project involving multiple algorithms, models, and large volumes of data may have a number of inherent design and implementation risks, each of which must be managed to ensure successful completion of the project.

In summary, a solutions architect should make sure to conduct a detailed risk assessment of the solutions architecture before finalizing it. Without proper risk assessment, the architecture of the solution and its related delivery plan may not be complete. This could lead to delays in the project, additional costs, and may even result in project failure. Conducting a detailed risk assessment helps the solutions architect to identify and mitigate potential risks before the project proceeds to design and implementation.

# Project Deliverables (Technology Architecture)

In the process of creating the solutions architecture for a digital solution, a solutions architect may create a variety of deliverables. Some of the typical ones are listed below. These deliverables can often be integrated or merged to form part of the same document, based on project requirements or organizational standards. The range and depth of each deliverable depend significantly on the project's scope, thus varying from one project to another. The organization's internal policies and methods can also influence the nature and form of these deliverables. Nevertheless, a few key deliverables are typically produced by a solutions architect while engaging with business stakeholders. Some of the typical deliverables include the following:

- **Solutions architecture design:** This is a comprehensive blueprint of the proposed solution, detailing the elements of the solution, their interrelationships, and the technology stack underpinning it all. This design provides an overarching view of the solution's structure and serves as a reference throughout the project's life cycle.

- **Technology stack:** This critical deliverable details the entire technology stack to be used in the solution. It includes every technology, programming language, framework, and tool that will be utilized in the development, deployment, and support of the solution. It often serves as a technical inventory and guides the developers' and system administrators' tasks.

- **Integration strategy:** This deliverable delineates a strategic plan for seamlessly integrating various solution components. It also covers integration with pre-existing systems, third-party services, and data sources. This strategy is crucial for ensuring interoperability and coordination across different parts of the solution.

- **Scalability and performance plan:** This deliverable provides a thorough analysis of the solution's scalability and its performance under varying workloads. It outlines strategies for load balancing, caching, resource optimization, and other techniques to ensure the system remains responsive and efficient even under peak loads.

- **Data architecture:** This is a detailed exposition of the system's data elements, their interrelationships, and their management protocols. It typically includes data models, data flow diagrams, and other related documentation that serve to guide the system's data handling practices.

- **Infrastructure and deployment strategy:** This detailed plan outlines the physical and virtual resources needed to support the system, such as servers, storage, and networking infrastructure. It includes information about the solution's deployment, maintenance, scaling strategies, and contingency measures to ensure the system remains reliable and resilient.

- **Technology maturity assessment:** This crucial deliverable helps explain the organization's current technical and business capabilities. It assesses these capabilities against industry best practices and identifies gaps that the new solution needs to address. This allows the solutions architect to prioritize changes and design a solution that aligns with the organization's strategic objectives while capitalizing on existing technology investments.

- **POC results:** The POC results offer vital insights into the solution's feasibility, performance, and potential hurdles. By detailing test scenarios, performance metrics, identified risks, and lessons learned, this deliverable enables informed decision-making regarding technology adoption and implementation strategies.

- **Security and compliance strategy:** This document outlines the security controls, policies, and procedures to be implemented in the solution to ensure compliance with applicable laws, regulations, and industry standards. It is crucial in maintaining the solution's integrity, confidentiality, and availability.

- **Disaster recovery and business continuity plan:** This vital document outlines strategies and procedures for recovering from system failures or disruptions, ensuring business operations continue with minimal disruption.

- **Testing and validation strategy:** This deliverable establishes a methodology for verifying the solution's functionality, performance, and reliability. It includes test scenarios, test cases, and acceptance criteria, providing a clear roadmap for quality assurance.

- **Monitoring and maintenance plan:** This strategy lays out a comprehensive plan for monitoring the solution's performance, diagnosing issues, and carrying out regular maintenance tasks to ensure its long-term stability and reliability.

In conclusion, these deliverables created by a solutions architect, constitute the backbone of a well-designed digital solution. They collectively ensure comprehensive understanding and efficient management of various aspects of the solution, from the technology stack and integration strategy to security protocols and maintenance plans. Each deliverable's depth and detail will depend on the project's scope and specific needs. However, they are all crucial to project success, and they often merge to form a comprehensive document serving as the project's blueprint.

# Summary

This chapter covered the topic of creating a digital solution's target architecture document, which identifies and defines all of a solution's critical components and establishes an integration strategy for the project as a whole. It serves as a high-level technical architecture for the project, guiding the technical design and development of the technical team. Maintaining the target architecture document is a continuous process that requires ongoing attention and refinement throughout the project's lifecycle to ensure a project's success.

The chapter also discussed various topics related to creating the target architecture document, including conducting a current state infrastructure and technology assessment, selecting technology stacks, conducting POCs and technical evaluations of tools and services, aligning with EA, developing the solution's target technology architecture, creating the application architecture, creating a data architecture, creating the security architecture, and assessing risks with the proposed architecture. The chapter also highlighted certain project deliverables that a solutions architect may create in this phase of the project. By following these steps and continually refining the target architecture document, the solutions architect can ensure the successful development and implementation of digital solutions.

# References

1. Kern, J. (2021, March 16). "How Tech Assessment Can Yield ROI." Forrester. Retrieved from www.forrester.com/blogs/how-tech-assessment-can-yield-roi-kenna-security/

2. Microsoft. (n.d.). Regulatory compliance dashboard. Azure Defender for Cloud. Retrieved from https://learn.microsoft.com/en-us/azure/defender-for-cloud/regulatory-compliance-dashboard

3. Heap. (n.d.). "What is a tech stack?" Heap. Retrieved from www.heap.io/topics/what-is-a-tech-stack

4. Day.IO. (January 11, 2022). "Proof of concept definition and why is it important." Day.IO Blog. Retrieved from https://day.io/blog/proof-of-concept-definition-and-why-is-it-important/

5. Ardoq. (July 5, 2021). "Enterprise architecture vs. solution architecture: What's the difference?" Ardoq Blog. Retrieved from www.ardoq.com/blog/enterprise-architecture-vs-solution-architecture

6. BMC Software, Inc. (2018). "Data Architecture vs. Information Architecture: What's the Difference?" Retrieved from www.bmc.com/blogs/data-architecture-vs-information-architecture/

7. Wikipedia contributors. (February 28, 2022). "Information architecture." In Wikipedia, The Free Encyclopedia. Retrieved 20:57, March 27, 2023, from https://en.wikipedia.org/wiki/Information_architecture

8. GitLab. (n.d.). "Security Architecture." *GitLab Handbook*. Retrieved from https://about.gitlab.com/handbook/security/architecture

9. National Institute of Standards and Technology (NIST). (2014). "Framework for Improving Critical Infrastructure Cybersecurity." NIST Cybersecurity Framework. Retrieved from www.govinfo.gov/content/pkg/GOVPUB-C13-00f462b8222d80a07feebd1f12ebfe4f/pdf/GOVPUB-C13-00f462b8222d80a07feebd1f12ebfe4f.pdf

# CHAPTER 5

# Deciding on Digital Architectural Frameworks and Best Practices

As organizations actively implement more new digital services on the cloud, they have the choice of using cloud services from different providers. AWS (Amazon Web Services), Azure (Microsoft Azure), and GCP (Google Cloud Platform) are three of the leading cloud service providers, each offering a range of competitive cloud services to organizations. Each cloud provider offers its own set of services and features, pricing models, and levels of security and compliance. Organizations select a cloud service provider that best meets their specific needs and requirements. In some cases, organizations may also use services from multiple providers to design and implement their digital solutions.

The wide range of options available for implementing digital solutions and their complexity can make the task of selecting the right services and options difficult. Even when an organization chooses to use one cloud provider, such as AWS, Azure, or GCP, there are still multiple options available from each of those providers to design and build solutions.

© Wasim Rajput 2023
W. Rajput, *Solutions Architecture*, https://doi.org/10.1007/978-1-4842-9657-8_5

Each cloud provider offers a wide range of digital and cloud services and features that can be used to build custom solutions that meet the organization's specific needs and requirements. Here are some examples:

- **Compute:** Within a single cloud provider, there are multiple options for compute services. For example, AWS offers EC2 (Elastic Compute Cloud), Elastic Beanstalk, Lambda (serverless computing), and more. Each of these services has its own benefits and limitations, and each can be used to build different types of applications. Similarly, GCP offers compute services such as Compute Engine for running VMs, Kubernetes Engine for containerized applications, and Cloud Functions for serverless computing.

- **Storage:** Similarly, within a single cloud provider, there are multiple options for storage services. For example, Azure offers several storage services, including Azure Blob Storage for unstructured data, Azure Files for SMB-based (Server Message Block) file shares, Azure Queue Storage for messaging between components, Azure Table Storage for NoSQL and large amounts of data, and Azure Disk Storage for persistent VM storage. GCP, on the other hand, offers Cloud Storage for object storage, Persistent Disk for block storage, and Filestore for file storage.

- **Databases:** Cloud providers offer multiple database services to meet different types of requirements. For example, AWS offers RDS (Relational Database Service) for managing traditional relational databases, DynamoDB for NoSQL databases, and Aurora for a managed relational database that is highly scalable.

In contrast, GCP provides Cloud SQL and Cloud Spanner for relational databases, Firestore and Firebase Realtime Database for NoSQL databases, and Bigtable for large operational databases.

- **Networking:** Cloud providers offer multiple networking services to manage network infrastructure in the cloud. For example, AWS offers VPC (Virtual Private Cloud) for creating isolated network environments, Direct Connect for establishing dedicated network connections to the cloud, and Route 53 for managing DNS (Domain Name System). Similarly, GCP provides VPC (Virtual Private Cloud) for network isolation, Cloud Interconnect for private connections to the cloud, and Cloud DNS for managing DNS.

- **Security:** Cloud providers offer multiple security services to help organizations secure their applications and data in the cloud. For example, AWS offers IAM (Identity and Access Management) for managing user access and permissions, AWS WAF (Web Application Firewall) for protecting web applications, and Shield for DDoS (distributed denial-of-service) protection. Meanwhile, GCP provides IAM (Identity and Access Management) for managing user access, Security Command Center for unified asset and security data view, and Cloud Armor for DDoS protection and web application firewall.

In summary, the extensive array and complexity of digital services offered by cloud providers such as AWS, Azure, and GCP present substantial challenges for organizations and solutions architects. The task of understanding, selecting, and integrating the right combination of services to create optimized solutions requires considerable expertise and strategic foresight. As you will observe in the next section, it necessitates the development and maintenance of robust, adaptable frameworks and standards within organizations to guide technological decisions.

# Why Choose an Architectural Framework?

As noted, cloud providers like AWS, Azure, and GCP offer a wide range of services in today's digital landscape. While these services provide opportunities for organizations, they also come with challenges due to the sheer number of options available. To navigate this complexity, organizations must establish clear standards as a compass for selecting digital solutions. These standards serve as guiding principles that help align choices with strategic objectives and ensure consistency in technological decisions.

Therefore, embracing a well-defined architectural framework empowered by clear standards can allow organizations to expedite their digital transformation journey and adapt to rapidly evolving market demands [1]. With strategic choices driven by these standards, decision-makers can confidently navigate the complex landscape of digital services, driving innovation and growth. Overall, establishing standards and employing a well-defined architectural framework can enable organizations to effectively leverage digital services, improving their operational efficiency, scalability, security, agility, and implementation speed in the dynamic digital landscape.

The following outlines some of the benefits of following an architectural framework and related standards and best practices.

- **Standardization:** Standardizing on certain design practices helps the development team make the right decisions more rapidly. When teams are familiar with best practices and guidelines, they can quickly take action without spending time exploring different options or resolving avoidable issues. Standardization also ensures consistency across different projects, leading to better outcomes and increased efficiency.

- **Narrowing down the focus:** Digital solutions often require the integration of multiple tools and technologies from various cloud providers, vendors, and other sources. Each of these tools and services typically comes with its own set of architectural guidelines, which can be challenging to navigate. A well-defined framework can help by providing clear guidance and best practices for each tool and technology, ensuring that the development team stays aligned with the overall architectural vision and meets the goals of the project.

- **Ensuring adherence to industry best practices:** By leveraging existing architectural frameworks provided by cloud and digital service providers, solutions architects can ensure adherence to industry best practices and trends. This not only helps in designing and implementing efficient and effective solutions but also aids in maintaining standardization of the design and architecture of digital systems.

In conclusion, adopting an architectural framework for solutions architecture is essential in today's multifaceted digital landscape. It provides organizations with a clear roadmap for making informed decisions and understanding the complexities of cloud services. By selecting the most suitable services aligned with strategic objectives, organizations can effectively implement digital solutions and improve operational efficiency, scalability, and security. The framework also promotes standardization and consistency, ensuring adherence to industry best practices. Embracing this comprehensive guide empowers organizations to thrive in their digital transformation journey while adapting to the ever-evolving technological landscape.

# Industry Digital Architectural Frameworks

Fortunately, many cloud and digital service providers, such as AWS, Azure, and GCP, as well as vendors of digital solutions offer architectural frameworks, which make this task easier. The use of these frameworks provides a set of best practices and guidelines to build efficient and effective solutions while ensuring standardization of the design and architecture of digital systems. By leveraging these frameworks, solutions architects can assist their teams in designing and implementing digital solutions while maintaining adherence to industry best practices and trends.

Here are some of the most widely used cloud architecture frameworks and architectures.

## Amazon Web Services Well-Architected Framework

The Amazon Web Services Well-Architected framework is a set of best practices and guidelines for building and running high-quality cloud infrastructure [2]. The framework provides a consistent approach to evaluating digital and cloud architectures and identifying areas for improvement. It is based on five pillars: operational excellence, security, reliability, performance efficiency, cost optimization, and sustainability. By following the framework's guidelines, organizations can improve the quality of their digital and cloud infrastructure, optimize costs, and reduce risk. The framework is continuously updated to incorporate new best practices and industry standards, ensuring that organizations always have access to the latest information and guidance for building and running cloud infrastructure on AWS.

# The Azure Well-Architected Framework

The Azure Well-Architected framework [3] is a set of best practices and guidelines for building and running high-quality cloud infrastructure on the Microsoft Azure cloud platform. The framework provides a structured approach to evaluating architectures and identifying areas for improvement based on five pillars: cost optimization, operational excellence, performance efficiency, reliability, security, and sustainability. By following the framework's guidelines, organizations can improve the quality of their cloud infrastructure, optimize costs, and reduce risk. The framework is continuously updated to incorporate new best practices and industry standards, ensuring that organizations always have access to the latest information and guidance for building and running cloud infrastructure on Azure.

# Google Cloud Architecture

The Google Cloud Architecture framework [4] is a set of best practices and guidelines for building and running high-quality cloud infrastructure on the Google Cloud Platform. The framework provides a consistent approach to evaluating architectures and identifying areas for improvement based on several pillars: operational excellence; security, privacy, and compliance; reliability; cost optimization; and performance optimization. The framework emphasizes the use of managed services and serverless computing to improve operational efficiency, as well as the use of open-source technologies and interoperability with other platforms.

By following the framework's guidelines, organizations can optimize their cloud infrastructure for performance, security, and cost-effectiveness, while leveraging the power and flexibility of the Google Cloud Platform. The framework is continuously updated to incorporate new best practices and industry standards, ensuring that organizations always have access to the latest information and guidance for building and running cloud infrastructure on Google Cloud.

# Cloud Native Computing Foundation Cloud Native Landscape

The Cloud Native Computing Foundation (CNCF) [5] is an open-source software foundation that aims to promote the adoption of cloud-native technologies and practices. The CNCF provides a neutral home for open-source projects related to containerization, microservices, and other cloud-native technologies. Its objective is to standardize these technologies and practices, making it easier for organizations to build and deploy cloud-native applications. By standardizing these technologies, the CNCF helps ensure that applications built using cloud-native tools can be easily deployed and run on a wide range of cloud platforms, making it easier for organizations to adopt and integrate new technologies. The CNCF also provides resources and support for organizations to help them adopt cloud-native technologies and practices, including training, certification, and community events. By leveraging the CNCF's resources and expertise, organizations can accelerate their adoption of cloud-native technologies and build more scalable, efficient, and resilient applications.

# CISA Internet of Things Acquisition Guidance

The Cybersecurity and Infrastructure Security Agency's "Internet of Things Acquisition Guidance" [6] provides recommendations and best practices for federal agencies and other organizations to consider when acquiring IoT devices and systems. The guidance covers various aspects of the acquisition process, including planning, procurement, and deployment, and it provides recommendations for managing security risks throughout the lifecycle of an IoT system. The guidance is intended to help organizations mitigate security risks associated with IoT devices and systems, which can be vulnerable to cyberattacks and other security threats if not properly secured.

# OpenStack Architecture

OpenStack [7] is an open-source cloud computing platform that enables users to build and manage their own cloud infrastructure. Its modular and flexible architecture consists of several core components, including Compute, Storage, Networking, Identity, and Dashboard, with optional components available. Users of this technology are typically organizations that require a customized cloud platform for their specific needs, such as enterprises, government agencies, and service providers. OpenStack allows users to have control over their cloud infrastructure and can provide cost savings compared to using public cloud providers.

# Kubernetes Architecture

Kubernetes, also known as K8s, is an open-source container orchestration system used for automating the deployment, scaling, and management of containerized applications [8]. It was originally developed by Google and is now maintained by the Cloud Native

Computing Foundation. Kubernetes provides a platform-agnostic way to deploy and manage containerized applications, enabling organizations to manage and scale containerized workloads across multiple cloud providers or on-premises data centers. Kubernetes offers several key features, including automatic scaling, self-healing, service discovery, and load balancing, making it a powerful tool for managing containerized applications in production environments. The site provides comprehensive documentation, tutorials, and resources for users and developers who want to learn about and use Kubernetes for container orchestration. The website offers detailed explanations of Kubernetes concepts and features, including architecture, API reference, cluster management, storage, networking, and security. Additionally, it provides installation guides and tools for various operating systems and cloud platforms, as well as community-contributed resources, such as blog posts, podcasts, and events. The website is a valuable resource for anyone interested in learning about Kubernetes or using it in their containerized application environments.

# Tanzu

Tanzu [9] is a portfolio of products and services from VMware that is designed to help organizations build, run, and manage modern applications and workloads across multi-cloud environments. Tanzu offers several tools and platforms that enable developers to build and deploy cloud-native applications, while also providing IT teams with tools for managing containers, Kubernetes, and other infrastructure components. Some of the products in the Tanzu portfolio include Tanzu Kubernetes Grid, which provides a multi-cloud Kubernetes runtime; Tanzu Mission Control, which provides centralized management and control for Kubernetes clusters across multiple clouds; and Tanzu

Application Service, which provides a platform for running and managing applications in a cloud-native environment. Tanzu is aimed at simplifying the complexity of modern application development and management, allowing organizations to focus on delivering innovative applications and services to their customers.

The aforementioned cloud computing and cloud-native architectures and frameworks are some of the popular ones that offer guidelines and tools that can help organizations design and operate digital and cloud-based systems that are scalable, secure, and cost-effective. It's important to carefully evaluate which framework best meets the organization's specific needs and digital solution requirements. Factors to consider include the type of applications being developed, the cloud platform in use, and the organization's security and compliance requirements.

# Example: AWS Well-Architected Framework

To gain a better understanding of an architectural framework, let's delve into the AWS Well-Architected framework, which is a popular architecture framework used for designing and operating cloud applications. While the scope of the framework is vast, and discussing each aspect in detail is beyond the scope of this book, I will cover some of the essential specifics. Detailed information on the framework can be downloaded from the AWS website.

# About the AWS Well-Architected Framework

The AWS Well-Architected framework is a collection of pillars, design practices, and architectural best practices that cloud architects can use to design and operate cloud applications. While the framework is designed specifically for applications and systems built using AWS services, many of its principles can be applied to other cloud platforms as well. The AWS Well-Architected framework provides a valuable tool for cloud architects looking to build and operate high-quality cloud applications.

# The Six Pillars of the AWS Well-Architected Framework

Amazon's Well-Architected framework is built on six architectural pillars.

1. **Operational excellence:** This pillar focuses on practices to run applications, monitor their performance, and continually improve related processes and procedures. Key topics include automation of operations, incident management and reporting, and continuous feedback-driven operational improvement.

2. **Performance efficiency:** This pillar focuses on practices related to ensuring optimal performance of systems. Topics covered include selecting the right resource types, capacity sizing, monitoring and tweaking systems for performance, and configuring and using the right dashboards for monitoring.

3. **Cost optimization:** This pillar focuses on topics related to cost optimization by ensuring that the appropriate number of resources is used to avoid incurring additional costs. Topics include monitoring costs, estimating costs, resource cost and usage analysis, and rightsizing recommendations.

4. **Security:** This pillar focuses on practices related to the protection of information, systems, data, and such. Key topics include protecting user confidentiality and integrity, identity and access management, infrastructure and data protection, and protection of data at rest and in transit.

5. **Reliability:** This pillar focuses on practices related to ensuring that systems are reliable and can recover from failures. Key topics include fault tolerance, recovery planning, and disaster recovery.

6. **Sustainability:** This pillar focuses on practices related to the efficient use of resources and reducing environmental impact. Key topics include power usage effectiveness and server utilization.

By following these pillars, architects can ensure that their applications are designed and operated in a way that is secure, reliable, efficient, and cost-effective, while also being environmentally sustainable. The Well-Architected framework is a valuable tool for cloud architects looking to build and operate high-quality cloud applications.

# Design Principles

Each pillar of the AWS framework includes a number of design principles. For example, the framework lists five key design principles under the operational excellence pillar. They are as follows:

- **Perform operations as code:** In the cloud, it's possible to implement the same engineering approach used for application code across the entire environment. This involves defining the whole workload, including applications and infrastructure as code, and updating it accordingly. Operational procedures can be scripted and their execution automated in response to specific events. By treating operations as code, the potential for human error is reduced and a consistent response to events is ensured.

- **Make frequent, small, reversible changes:** This design principle is about creating workloads that allow for regular component updates, thus enabling the integration of required changes. Implementing small, reversible changes facilitates the identification and resolution of any issues that may arise in the environment, while striving to minimize negative impact on customers and the overall environment.

- **Refine operations procedures frequently:** This design practice focuses on continuously refining operational procedures by seeking out improvement opportunities. As the workload evolves, procedures should be adapted to match the workloads. This practice encourages the review and verification of the efficacy of procedures while familiarizing teams with their execution.

- **Anticipate failure:** This design practice is about conducting "pre-mortem" exercises to pinpoint potential failure sources and to remove or mitigate them accordingly. It involves testing various failure scenarios, as well as verifying the effectiveness of response procedures and ensuring that teams are well-versed in their execution.

- **Learn from all operational failures:** This design practice is about enabling improvement by deriving lessons from all operational events and failures. It emphasizes the importance of sharing these lessons across teams and throughout the entire organization to enhance overall performance.

# Best Practices

Each architectural pillar also includes a number of best practices related to various categories. For the operational excellence pillar, although there are numerous best practices mentioned within each pillar, here are some to illustrate them.

- **Evaluate external customer needs:** This best practice is about involving key stakeholders from business, development, and operations teams to prioritize external customer needs. In doing so, one can get a comprehensive understanding of the operational support required for achieving desired business outcomes.

- **Evaluate internal customer needs:** This best practice involves collaborating with key internal stakeholders across business, development, and operations teams to address internal customer needs effectively. By understanding the operational support required for various business outcomes, improvements can be strategically focused on areas such as team skills, workload performance, cost reduction, automation, or monitoring.

- **Perform patch management:** This best practice is
  about implementing patch management to acquire
  features, resolve issues, and maintain compliance with
  governance. Automating patch management minimizes
  errors caused by manual processes and reduces the
  effort required for patching. This practice encourages
  the use of immutable infrastructures wherever possible
  but if that's not feasible, in-place patching remains
  an alternative option. Immutable infrastructure is
  an approach to managing IT infrastructure where
  components are replaced rather than updated,
  ensuring a consistent and stable environment by
  eliminating changes to existing systems.

- **Implement practices to improve code quality:**
  This best practice centers on adopting practices that
  enhance code quality and minimize defects, such as
  utilizing test-driven development, conducting code
  reviews, and implementing coding standards.

- **Fully automate integration and deployment:** This
  best practice emphasizes automating the build,
  deployment, and testing processes of the workload,
  which helps decrease errors resulting from manual
  procedures and lowers the effort needed to implement
  changes.

# AWS Well-Architected Lenses

AWS Well-Architected provides general guidance for building and
operating cloud-based systems. However, Amazon recognizes that
specific use cases may require tailored approaches. To address these
unique scenarios, Amazon has introduced "lenses," which are specialized

adaptations of the Well-Architected framework for particular types of applications or technologies. For example, the Container Build Lens is a specific set of architectural principles, guidelines, and best practices designed to optimize container-based applications. AWS also offers lenses for data analytics, SAP applications, serverless applications, hybrid networking, and others.

In summary, lenses allow the application of AWS Well-Architected framework to specific situations in a more focused manner.

# Deciding on a Custom Architectural Framework

While established industry architectural frameworks provide useful guidance and best practices for solutions architecture, solutions architects may find it beneficial to develop their own custom framework tailored to their organization's specific needs and requirements. This is because established frameworks can be lengthy and may not provide a clear, focused approach to address the specific challenges and objectives of the organization. Developing a custom framework allows solutions architects to create a streamlined and targeted approach to solutions architecture that is tailored to the organization's needs.

Creating a custom framework involves assessing the organization's current needs, goals, and priorities and then identifying the key factors that should be considered in the solutions architecture process. This can include factors such as the organization's business strategy, technology goals, regulatory requirements, and existing IT infrastructure. By identifying these factors, solutions architects can create a framework that addresses specific areas of concern, ensuring that the solutions architecture aligns with the organization's overall objectives.

# Example: Selecting the Right Kubernetes Service

As an example, let's look at Kubernetes, which has become the standard way of managing containerized workloads and has grown in popularity in recent years. Organizations can choose from a variety of options for implementing Kubernetes, ranging from DIY (Do It Yourself) approaches to fully managed solutions offered by cloud providers. Let's explore the options that a solutions architect may have and the factors that may influence their decision.

## Self-Managed Kubernetes

Organizations can choose to set up and manage their own Kubernetes clusters using open-source tools such as Kubernetes, Kubeadm, and Helm. This approach gives them full control over the deployment, configuration, and management of their Kubernetes environment. However, it requires significant expertise and resources to manage a Kubernetes cluster effectively. The organization needs to manage the underlying infrastructure, including servers, storage, and networking, as well as ensuring the cluster is highly available, secure, and scalable. This approach is suitable for organizations that have a dedicated team with expertise in Kubernetes, have specific requirements that cannot be met by managed solutions, or have a preference for complete control over their environment.

## Managed Kubernetes Services

Cloud providers like Amazon Web Services and Microsoft Azure offer fully managed Kubernetes services such as Amazon Elastic Kubernetes Service (Amazon EKS) and Azure Kubernetes Service (AKS), respectively. Google Kubernetes Engine (GKE) Autopilot is a mode of operation in

Google Kubernetes Engine where Google Cloud automatically manages and operates the underlying Kubernetes infrastructure, including the control plane and the worker nodes. This allows developers and operators to focus more on deploying and managing their applications, and less on managing and operating the underlying infrastructure. This approach allows organizations to deploy and manage Kubernetes clusters without the overhead of infrastructure management. The cloud provider handles the underlying infrastructure, including servers, storage, and networking, while the organization focuses on deploying its applications and services. Managed Kubernetes services also provide built-in features such as automatic scaling, load balancing, and security features. However, this approach may limit the organization's flexibility and control over the environment, as it must rely on the cloud provider's offerings and capabilities. Managed Kubernetes services are suitable for organizations that want to focus on their applications and services and reduce the operational overhead of managing infrastructure.

## Kubernetes as a Service

Kubernetes as a Service (KaaS) providers like Platform9, Mirantis, and Giant Swarm offer fully managed Kubernetes environments on their own infrastructure. This approach allows organizations to deploy and manage Kubernetes clusters without the overhead of managing infrastructure or relying on a cloud provider's capabilities. KaaS providers often offer additional services, such as continuous integration and delivery (CI/CD), monitoring, and logging, to provide a complete solution for deploying and managing containerized workloads. However, this approach may limit the organization's flexibility and control over the environment, as it must rely on the KaaS provider's offerings and capabilities. KaaS is suitable for organizations that want a turnkey solution for deploying and managing containerized workloads and don't want to manage the infrastructure or rely on a cloud provider's capabilities.

## Hybrid Approach

Organizations can also choose a hybrid approach, combining self-managed Kubernetes with managed Kubernetes or KaaS services. For example, an organization can choose to manage its Kubernetes environment on-premises or in a private cloud, while using managed Kubernetes services like Amazon EKS or AKS for their public cloud deployments. This approach provides greater flexibility and control over the environment while reducing the operational overhead of managing infrastructure. However, it also requires the organization to manage and integrate multiple Kubernetes environments, which may increase complexity and costs.

By weighing the pros and cons of each option, solutions architects can select the service that best matches the organization's goals and objectives and also provides a clear, focused approach to solution development and implementation.

# Technical Debt Considerations in Solutions Architecture

In this section, you will delve into the concept of technical debt, exploring its implications on software and digital systems and, more importantly, how it intertwines with the role of solutions architects. You will examine the various ways in which architectural decisions can contribute to or exacerbate technical debt and provide insights on strategic approaches that solutions architects can adopt to minimize its accumulation. The section will highlight the importance of establishing standards and frameworks that promote best practices to help mitigate the risk of accumulating technical debt. By implementing robust guidelines and architectural principles, solutions architects can proactively address potential debt and ensure long-term software maintainability.

# Technical Debt and Its Relevance to Solutions Architecture

Technical debt is a concept in software development that reflects the implied cost of additional rework caused by choosing an easy or quick solution now instead of using a better approach that would take longer. The term can also include outdated technology, poor documentation, lack of testing, and sloppy coding practices. It was coined by Ward Cunningham [10] to describe the long-term costs and consequences of expedited software development.

Here's how technical debt can impact an organization:

- **Reduced productivity:** If an organization has a lot of technical debt, its developers may spend more time fixing bugs and issues than adding new features or improving the system. This decreases productivity and slows down the pace of innovation.

- **Increased costs:** As technical debt accumulates, it can lead to significant financial costs. This includes the direct costs of paying developers to fix issues and the indirect costs of lost productivity and opportunity costs.

- **Poor quality products:** When technical debt leads to bugs, crashes, or performance issues, it can degrade the quality of the product or service that the organization provides. This can lead to customer dissatisfaction and potentially loss of market share.

- **Low morale:** Working in a codebase with high technical debt can be frustrating and demoralizing for developers. This can lead to lower job satisfaction and higher turnover, which can further increase costs and reduce productivity.

- **Strategic risk:** In the long term, high technical debt can put an organization's strategic goals at risk. If the organization's systems are unstable or hard to change, it can be difficult to adapt to new market opportunities or threats.

- **Scalability issues:** High technical debt can hinder scalability efforts. As the system grows and evolves, the debt (if not dealt with properly) can make it increasingly difficult to implement necessary changes or enhancements, affecting the overall growth of the organization.

Although the concept of technical debt is a concept that originates in software development, it's also applicable to other systems and processes in an organization. It's not limited to poor software alone; it can occur anytime a suboptimal or expedited decision is made with the intent to correct or improve it later. Here are some examples.

- **Infrastructure debt:** The choice to use outdated or cheaper hardware, or not following best practices in infrastructure setup, can lead to infrastructure technical debt. This can result in performance and reliability issues that can disrupt business operations, negatively impact customer experience, and require expensive hardware upgrades and restructuring in the future.

- **Data debt:** Poorly designed databases, lack of data governance, or ineffective data quality controls can result in data-related technical debt. This can impede an organization's capacity to use its data efficiently for decision-making or operations, creating inefficiencies and potential inaccuracies in business processes that rely heavily on data. Correcting these issues later can require substantial effort and resources.

- **Process debt:** When business processes are hastily designed or implemented without optimization, the organization incurs what can be referred to as process debt. This can lead to inefficient or overly complex processes that slow down operations, reduce productivity, and potentially create customer dissatisfaction. Over time, the organization will need to invest in redesigning these processes to improve efficiency and effectiveness.

- **Information security debt:** Ignoring or delaying best practices in security for the sake of expedience can create a form of technical debt that increases the organization's vulnerability to cyber threats. This can lead to significant business disruptions in the event of a security breach and may require extensive remediation efforts.

As you can see, the impact of technical debt on various system dimensions can have far-reaching effects on an organization's overall business operations. It can lead to inefficiencies, increased costs, and disruptions that adversely affect an organization's ability to deliver its products or services effectively.

The concept of technical debt, therefore, is a critical concern for technical teams, particularly in today's fast-paced digital solutions delivery environments. Well-thought-out technical standards and architectural frameworks can provide a pathway to balance this challenge. These standards and frameworks, when effectively implemented, guide teams to design and build solutions that not only meet immediate requirements but also consider future needs and scalability. This approach ensures that teams can maintain development speed without sacrificing the quality of their work. Over time, adhering to these standards can result in less technical debt, or even reduce existing debt, as it discourages short-term fixes and encourages solutions built for long-term stability and maintainability. This harmonization of speed and quality can lead to more efficient development cycles and robust solutions, ultimately benefiting the teams, the end users, and the organization as a whole. Figure 5-1 illustrates this balance.

***Figure 5-1.*** *Balancing immediate delivery pressures with quality of delivery*

Therefore, managing technical debt is crucial for maintaining smooth and efficient business operations and ensuring the long-term success of an organization. To effectively manage and reduce technical debt, organizations and solutions architects should ensure that their decisions in the project lifecycle consider this concept. You will review that next.

## The Role of the Solutions Architect in Influencing Technical Debt

Solutions architects in their strategic role can greatly influence an organization's level of technical debt. Their decisions can either mitigate or exacerbate potential future issues that may arise from the accumulation of this debt. However, their ability to strike the right balance between speed and quality can be significantly enhanced by established standards, well-thought-out practices, and effective frameworks.

Established standards in software development provide a blueprint for quality and consistency. They include guidelines for code structure, commenting, naming conventions, and more. Following these standards can help prevent the creation of error-prone or hard-to-maintain code, which often contributes to technical debt. Solutions architects, by advocating for and ensuring adherence to these standards, can play a significant role in reducing the potential for this form of debt.

Similarly, well-thought-out practices, such as Test-Driven Development (TDD) or Pair Programming, can contribute to the quality of the software. By incorporating these practices into the development process, solutions architects can foster an environment that encourages writing robust, maintainable code, thus minimizing the risk of incurring technical debt.

Frameworks, on the other hand, provide structure and reusable components that can expedite the digital system's design and development process while maintaining quality. Solutions architects can also use standards, practices, and frameworks as reference points when making critical decisions. These elements provide a roadmap that architects can use to balance the need for speed in delivery with the requirement to "do things right." For instance, knowing the standard or framework's capabilities and limitations can inform decisions about whether a quick fix now would likely result in significant rework later.

In conclusion, solutions architects have a pivotal role in influencing the level of technical debt within an organization. The effectiveness of their decisions can, therefore, be significantly enhanced by established standards, well-thought-out practices, and effective frameworks. These tools can help architects navigate the often challenging balance between delivering quickly and ensuring long-term system sustainability and quality.

# Example: Technical Debt-Related Decisions

Let's consider a practical example of a digital project where a bank is planning to develop a new mobile banking application that is user-friendly, secure, and can handle a large volume of transactions.

The solutions architect in charge has the following key decisions to make that will influence the system's design and the potential for accumulating technical debt:

- **Choice of technology stack:** The solutions architect has to decide the technology stack to be used for the project. They might be tempted to adopt a new, cutting-edge technology for its advanced features and potential performance benefits. However, if the team lacks experience with this technology, this can result in suboptimal implementation and a steeper learning curve, introducing technical debt. Alternatively, using a familiar but possibly outdated technology might expedite the initial development but could accrue technical debt in the long run due to lower performance, diminished community support, or difficulty integrating with other modern systems. To make an informed decision, the architect could evaluate the team's proficiency with proposed technologies and the support available for these technologies in terms of community, documentation, and longevity. They might choose a newer technology if they judge that the team can quickly upskill and the long-term benefits outweigh the initial learning curve.

- **Code quality and standards:** When it comes to maintaining code quality and implementing coding standards, the solutions architect plays a crucial role. If the emphasis is on quick delivery, the team might overlook best practices like writing clean, modular code or following TDD. This can lead to a messy, bug-prone codebase that is harder to maintain and update in the future, thereby incurring technical debt. To navigate this, the architect might advocate for adherence to established coding standards and practices to ensure a robust, maintainable codebase. They could decide to provide training to the team on these practices and may argue for slightly extended development timeframes to accommodate these quality practices, considering their future benefits in reducing maintenance effort and error rates.

- **Security considerations:** Security is of paramount importance in banking applications. The architect might face a decision between implementing robust, time-consuming security measures upfront or launching quickly with minimal security, planning to enhance it later. The latter approach, while faster, could lead to significant security-related technical debt. The architect should emphasize the importance of thorough security measures given the sensitive nature of banking data. They might decide to invest time and resources upfront in implementing strong security features, such as encryption, secure APIs, and robust authentication mechanisms, to avoid future security risks and potential remediation efforts.

- **Scalability:** The solutions architect needs to consider the application's ability to handle growth in user traffic or data volume. They might be faced with a decision between a simpler, faster-to-implement architecture that may struggle under high loads, or a more complex, distributed architecture that scales well but might take longer to develop. Choosing the former can lead to scalability-related technical debt. In this case, the architect could consider the projected growth of the application. If high scalability is a likely requirement, they might decide to invest in a scalable architecture upfront, despite the additional initial development time, to avoid performance issues down the line.

- **User interface (UI) development:** The solutions architect has to decide between building a custom UI, which gives more control over the user experience but can be time-consuming, or using a ready-made UI framework to expedite development. The latter choice could accelerate the initial development, but potential limitations of the framework might lead to debt if extensive customizations become necessary later. The architect could consider the unique UI requirements of the project and the team's proficiency with the chosen framework. If the UI needs are complex or unique, they might decide to invest in a custom UI, despite the additional effort, to avoid future rework.

In each decision, the solutions architect needs to balance immediate needs with potential future costs associated with technical debt, guiding the project towards long-term success.

# Summary

This chapter highlighted the importance of using digital architectural frameworks for building digital solutions. These frameworks are based on industry-established best practices, standards, and guidelines that ensure alignment with the latest technological advancements. By leveraging these frameworks, solutions architects can ensure that digital solutions are designed, implemented, and managed in a way that aligns with industry standards.

As digital technologies and trends continue to evolve, organizations must adapt quickly and efficiently to these changes. By following industry frameworks, they can ensure that the frameworks are kept up to date by their owners.

I delved into the concept of technical debt, an essential consideration when implementing digital solutions. I emphasized that well-thought-out standards and architectural frameworks are key in preventing technical debt. By adhering to industry standards and using robust architectural frameworks, organizations can ensure that the solutions they implement are both scalable and maintainable.

Finally, I covered the importance of organizations customizing these frameworks to their specific needs and ensuring that they align with their overall business strategy. A one-size-fits-all approach may not always be appropriate for every organization, and they may need to tailor the frameworks to fit their unique requirements. Additionally, organizations should regularly review and update these frameworks to ensure that they remain relevant and effective in the face of changing technologies and business needs.

# References

1. Avolution. (2021, July 8). "How to Choose an Enterprise Architecture Framework. Avolution Software." Retrieved from www.avolutionsoftware. com/news/how-to-choose-an-enterprise-architecture-framework/

2. Amazon Web Services (AWS). (n.d.). Well-Architected. AWS Architecture Center. Retrieved from https://aws.amazon.com/architecture/well-architected

3.  www.microsoft.com/azure/partners/well-architected

4.  https://cloud.google.com/architecture/framework

5.  www.cncf.io/

6.  www.cisa.gov/sites/default/files/publications/20_0204_cisa_sed_internet_of_things_acquisition_guidance_final_508_1.pdf

7.  https://docs.openstack.org/arch-design/

8.  Kubernetes - Production-Grade Container Orchestration. Retrieved March 31, 2023, from https://kubernetes.io/

9.  https://tanzu.vmware.com/tanzu

10. "What is technical debt?" TechTarget. Retrieved June 7, 2023, from www.techtarget.com/whatis/definition/technical-debt

CHAPTER 6

# Concluding Remarks for CIOs and Solutions Architects

This concluding chapter offers a few words for CIOs and CTOs, explaining the importance of the role of solutions architecture in delivering high-performing digital solutions that align with business goals and objectives. It is essential for CIOs and other technology executives to understand the value of this domain and how solutions architects can help their organizations to achieve their digital transformation goals. Toward the end, the chapter also reviews some of the key skills and knowledge needed to become a successful solutions architect.

## A Message to CIOs and CTOs

The role of a CIO or CTO is to ensure the delivery of digital and IT capabilities that are aligned with the business. They need to ensure that technology is integrated into the business and is not seen as a separate entity. To achieve this, they need to ensure alignment at all levels of the organization and ensure that all levels of their tech organizations are engaged in activities that maximize this alignment.

This alignment between technology and business has been a critical issue for CIOs and CTOs for several decades, as it's crucial to ensure that digital and IT capabilities are aligned with the business strategies, goals, and objectives. However, due to the constant evolution of technology, changing business needs, organizational silos, and such, executives continue to struggle with it.

One of the key reasons why achieving alignment can be challenging is due to the misconception that alignment is exclusively focused on higher levels of the organization. This misconception often overlooks the importance of alignment across all levels of the business and technology teams. Recognizing and addressing this misconception is the first step towards creating a culture of alignment that permeates throughout the entire organization.

This culture of alignment should not only exist amongst the teams but also reflect in the strategic approach of the organization's leaders. CIOs and CTOs, therefore, must take a holistic approach that encompasses both the business and technology aspects of the organization. They need to understand the business goals, objectives, and processes and then ensure that technology initiatives are tailored to meet them. By anticipating future needs while addressing current ones, leaders demonstrate their deep understanding of the business, its customers, and its markets. This holistic alignment, however, cannot be achieved without addressing one vital aspect of the organization: the domain of solutions architecture. This domain acts as the glue binding business goals with technology capabilities, serving as a conduit to truly achieving alignment.

# Ensuring Alignment Through the Domain of Solutions Architecture

As emphasized earlier in this book, the realm of solutions architecture plays a crucial role in ensuring the harmonious integration of digital solutions with business strategies, goals, and objectives. This is accomplished through the utilization of a well-defined framework that provides guidance for the design and execution of digital solutions. These solutions are custom tailored to not only address the unique requirements of the business but also take into account the technical implications and prerequisites.

At the core of solutions architecture lies the creation and implementation of purpose-built, scalable, and maintainable digital solutions. This necessitates a deep comprehension of the business context and requirements, which are subsequently translated into a technical architecture specifically tailored to fulfill those particular needs. The ultimate objective is to develop a solution that effectively bridges the divide between business requirements and technological capabilities, thereby fostering alignment within the organization.

# The Role of Solutions Architects

The role of solutions architects, thus, has become increasingly important in ensuring this alignment between digital solutions and business strategies, goals, and objectives. They are instrumental in providing and facilitating that alignment both at lower levels and by connecting at higher levels of the organization. CIOs and CTOs should empower them for ensuring that digital solutions are aligned with business strategies, goals, and objectives, and this requires collaboration across all levels of the organization.

At the lower levels of the organization, solutions architects work closely with the development teams to ensure that digital solutions are designed and implemented in a way that meets the requirements of the business. They provide guidance on technical design decisions, ensure that solutions are scalable and maintainable, and work to ensure that solutions are aligned with the overall architecture of the organization. By doing so, they help to ensure that digital solutions are designed and implemented in a way that supports the goals of the business.

At the same time, solutions architects also connect with higher levels of the organization, including senior management and business leaders. They work to understand the business strategy and goals, and they ensure that digital solutions are aligned with those goals. They provide guidance on the technical implications of business decisions and work to ensure that digital solutions are designed to support the long-term strategic goals of the organization.

In addition, solutions architects also facilitate alignment across different functional areas of the organization. They work to ensure that digital solutions are designed to support the needs of different business functions and that these solutions are integrated in a way that supports overall organizational objectives. They work to break down silos between different functional areas of the organization and ensure that digital solutions are designed to support cross-functional collaboration and communication.

Given the critical role solutions architects play in facilitating alignment throughout the organization, it is crucial for CIOs and CTOs to establish a robust solutions architecture team that possesses a comprehensive understanding of both IT and business requirements. These architects should be empowered to collaborate closely with business executives and IT teams, guiding the design and implementation of solutions that align with the overarching business strategy. By investing in skilled solutions architecture professionals, CIOs and CTOs can guarantee that their organizations have the necessary expertise to deliver impactful digital solutions while ensuring alignment between IT and business objectives.

# Becoming a Solutions Architect

In this section, I address a common question posed by many technical professionals interested in becoming digital solutions architects: "What are the necessary skills needed for this role?" To answer this effectively, let's begin by defining the term "solutions architect" and then cover some of the key skills required to thrive in this role.

# Definition of a Solutions Architect

First, it is important to note that there is no set definition of a solutions architect, and the role can vary significantly depending on the organization and its specific needs. In some organizations, a solutions architect may be seen as a highly technical position, with a strong focus on software development languages and programming expertise. This type of solutions architect is often responsible for designing and implementing complex software systems (working more or less as a software architect), using their deep understanding of software architecture and programming languages to create efficient and effective solutions.

In other organizations, the focus of the solutions architect may be on broader technical concepts, such as cloud computing and AWS/Azure/GCP architectural concepts. These solutions architects may be responsible for designing and implementing solutions that leverage the benefits of cloud computing, such as scalability, security, performance, cost effectiveness, and agility. They may work closely with development teams and stakeholders to understand business requirements and develop solutions that meet those needs.

Some organizations may even use the term "solutions architect" to refer to a more general technical leadership role, with a focus on providing high-level technical direction and guidance to teams and stakeholders.

Therefore, the focus area that a solutions architect pursues will depend on their own interests and expertise as well as the needs of the organization they work for. Some solutions architects may choose to focus on software development and programming languages, while others may focus on cloud computing and AWS/Azure/GCP architectural concepts. Ultimately, the role of a solutions architect is to design and implement solutions that meet business requirements and constraints, while leveraging their technical expertise and leadership skills to guide development teams and stakeholders towards a successful outcome.

# Key Skills Needed to Become a Solutions Architect

Even though the definition of a solutions architect may vary depending on the organization, there are still several skills that all solutions architects should possess. These skills are covered below.

## Technical Expertise

A solutions architect must have a deep understanding of technical concepts to design and implement solutions that meet business needs. Depending on the projects and the organizations, and how the role is defined, the required skills may include programming languages such as Java, Python, or C++, system architecture and design patterns, knowledge of cloud computing frameworks such as AWS or Azure, database design and management, networking protocols and security, DevOps practices and tools, API design and implementation, microservices architecture, security practices and tools, and agile methodologies. A combination of these technical skills enables solutions architects to design and implement effective solutions that meet business requirements and constraints.

## Business Alignment Skills

As discussed earlier in the book, one of the key domains of responsibility of a solutions architect is to work closely with the business to ensure business alignment. Such skills require solutions architects to gain a deeper understanding of the business and industry they are working in. They must be able to understand the organization's strategy, its strategic goals and objectives, and align technical solutions with that strategy and goals. Accordingly, they must be able to identify and prioritize business needs and requirements of the organization and then use their technical expertise to envision, design, develop, and implement solutions that address those needs and requirements.

Achieving this business alignment requires solutions architects to be able to work closely with the organization's business stakeholders. These stakeholders include business leaders, project managers, business users, development and operations teams. They must also be able to communicate technical concepts to non-technical stakeholders and help them understand the implications of technical decisions on the organization's business objectives, processes, business rules, and the overall business ecosystem. In doing so, solutions architects must be able to strike a balance between technical feasibility and the business needs and constraints.

## Ability to Envision the Technical Solution

As discussed earlier in the book, developing a vision for the technical solution and how its components integrate and fit together is a critical skill that solutions architects need to possess to be able to be effective in their roles. It involves envisioning a digital solution with technical capabilities that addresses the business requirements and user needs. Creating this vision is critical as it helps ensure that all stakeholders have a shared understanding of what the solution will deliver, how it will work, and how it will deliver the intended business outcomes.

Developing the ability to envision technical solutions is often the product of extensive experience with similar projects and a deep understanding of diverse technologies and their applications. Solutions architects with a rich history of implementing technical solutions are naturally better positioned to design such strategies, compared to those less experienced.

## Digital/IT Management Skills

Solutions architects should also possess good IT governance skills for them to be able to work effectively and deliver digital solutions and business outcomes. IT governance provides a framework for managing and controlling IT resources, ensuring that they are used effectively and efficiently to create value for the organization. Solutions architects with good IT governance skills are better equipped to design and implement effective technology solutions that deliver business value as well as comply with legal and regulatory requirements. They are able to work within the organization's IT governance frameworks to ensure that technology solutions are aligned with business objectives, manage IT-related risks, and optimize IT investments. By doing so, solutions architects can help organizations achieve their strategic goals and create long-term value.

## Enterprise Architecture Skills

As a solutions architect, familiarity with enterprise architecture (EA) is crucial. EA offers a structured approach to designing technology solutions, taking into account the organization's people, processes, information, and various technology dimensions. Understanding EA is important because it provides a holistic and strategic framework for designing and managing technology solutions. With this knowledge, a solutions architect can gain a deeper understanding of how the technology solutions they are working on align with the broader context of an organization's business strategy and goals.

Furthermore, learning about EA helps a solutions architect identify and manage risks and dependencies that could impact the success of technology solutions. As mentioned, EA provides a framework for analyzing the impact of changes to technology solutions on an organization's overall business operations, ensuring compliance with legal and regulatory requirements.

In summary, knowledge of EA enables the architect to design solutions that align with the organization's business objectives, effectively manage risks and dependencies, and communicate with other stakeholders. By leveraging EA, solutions architects can ensure that their technology solutions not only address specific needs but also align with the overall strategic direction of the organization.

# Building Professional Networks

To succeed as a solutions architect, it's essential to build professional relationships with various stakeholders, including business leaders, developers, project managers, and other stakeholders, both within and outside the organization. Solutions architects need to work closely with these stakeholders to ensure the successful implementation of technology solutions.

By building a network of professional relationships, for example, solutions architects can gain valuable insights into the industry, stay up to date with the latest trends and technologies, and uncover new opportunities for their organization. This includes staying in touch with vendors who provide access to specialized knowledge and expertise related to specific technologies and products.

Regular communication with vendors allows solutions architects to stay informed about product updates, enhancements, and emerging technologies that could potentially enhance their solutions. Additionally, vendors often offer support, training, and resources that can assist solutions architects in designing and implementing effective solutions.

To build and nurture their network, solutions architects can attend industry events, participate in meetups, connect with other professionals on platforms like LinkedIn, and seek mentorship opportunities from experienced professionals. By actively engaging with stakeholders, including vendors, solutions architects can expand their reach, collaborate effectively, and stay relevant in an ever-changing industry while leveraging the expertise and resources provided by all parties involved.

# Solutions Architecture Certifications

Certifications are an important aspect of becoming a solutions architect because they provide a tangible measure of a candidate's knowledge, skills, and expertise in a specific technology or field. For example, certifications such as AWS Certified Solutions Architect or Microsoft Certified: Azure Solutions Architect demonstrate a candidate's proficiency in designing and implementing solutions using specific cloud platforms.

Certifications can also serve as a form of professional development and help candidates stay up to date with the latest technologies and trends in the industry. For instance, the TOGAF 9 certification provides a framework for enterprise architecture that can be used to guide the design and implementation of technology solutions in a structured and systematic manner.

Furthermore, certifications in one area can be beneficial in others, especially if there is commonality of topics between the certifications. For example, a solutions architect certified in AWS cloud technologies may be able to transition to Azure easily because both platforms share concepts such as virtual machines, storage, networking, and security. Similarly, a solutions architect certified in VMware technologies may have an easier time learning about virtualization in cloud platforms such as AWS or Azure.

In conclusion, certifications are an important factor for evaluating a candidate for a solutions architect role, but they are not the only factor. Other elements, such as experience, soft skills, and the ability to think strategically and creatively are also important considerations. Additionally, certifications in one area can be beneficial in others, especially if there is commonality of topics between the certifications.

# Gaining Real-World Experience

The best way to build one's skills as a solutions architect is to gain real-world experience. Working on projects that align with one's career goals and utilizing technical knowledge and skills can lead to valuable experience. Roles such as a technical leads, systems analysis, or technical project managers can provide exposure to various technologies and industry verticals. Freelance projects and consulting work are also excellent opportunities to gain practical experience and develop skills in a practical setting. By participating in real-world projects, you can improve skills, gain practical experience, and build a portfolio that showcases their work. As a solutions architect, it is imperative to continually develop skills and expertise, and gaining real-world experience is an effective way to achieve that.

## The Importance of Soft Skills

Finally, in addition to technical skills, soft skills are also essential for solutions architects. Solutions architects need to communicate effectively with different stakeholders, including business leaders, developers, and project managers. They must be able to understand and translate technical concepts into language that non-technical stakeholders can understand. Solutions architects also need to be strong problem solvers, critical thinkers, and able to work well under pressure. They must be able to manage and prioritize multiple projects and deadlines effectively. Additionally, solutions architects need to have strong leadership and interpersonal skills, as they are often responsible for leading development teams and collaborating with other departments within the organization. Strong soft skills can help solutions architects build effective relationships with stakeholders, inspire confidence in their teams, and drive successful project outcomes.

# Summary

In conclusion, this chapter highlighted the critical role that the solutions architecture domain plays in bridging the gap between digital solutions and business strategies, goals, and objectives. A crucial takeaway is the importance of achieving alignment across all levels of the organization, and not just at the top. This alignment, facilitated by skilled solutions architects, is instrumental in delivering effective, scalable, and maintainable digital solutions that are in harmony with business needs.

CIOs and CTOs bear the responsibility of fostering this culture of alignment, requiring a deep understanding of both the business and technological aspects of the organization. Simultaneously, the value of a robust solutions architecture team cannot be overstated. These professionals, equipped with a comprehensive understanding of IT and business requirements, help ensure that digital solutions align with business strategies, goals, and objectives. Furthermore, this chapter underscored the important skills and knowledge required to excel as a solutions architect, providing guidance for those interested in stepping into this critical role. In essence, the journey towards successful digital transformation hinges on the effective integration of business needs with technological capabilities, facilitated by the pivotal role of solutions architecture.

# Index

Printed in the United States
by Baker & Taylor Publisher Services